Doubleday Short Studies in Politica

The Role of the Military
in American Foreign Policy

By BURTON M. SAPIN
and RICHARD C. SNYDER
Princeton University

DOUBLEDAY & COMPANY, INC.
Garden City, N.Y.
1954

LIBRARY OF CONGRESS CATALOG CARD NUMBER 54-8390
PRINTED IN THE UNITED STATES OF AMERICA
AT THE COUNTRY LIFE PRESS, GARDEN CITY, N.Y.

The Role of the Military
in American Foreign Policy

DOUBLEDAY SHORT STUDIES IN POLITICAL SCIENCE
Consulting Editor
Richard C. Snyde
Associate Professor of Politics, Princeton University

Spring, 1954

The Revolution in American Foreign Policy, 1945–1954
By William G. Carleton, Professor of Political Science and Head Professor of the Social Sciences, University of Florida

Political Community at the International Level: Problems of Definition and Measurement
By Karl W. Deutsch, Professor of History and Political Science, Massachusetts Institute of Technology

France: Keystone of Western Defense
By Edgar S. Furniss, Jr., Assistant Professor of Politics, Princeton University

The Problem of Internal Security in Great Britain, 1948–1953
By H. H. Wilson, Associate Professor of Politics, Princeton University and Harvey Glickman, Fellow, Harvard University

Germany: Dilemma for American Foreign Policy
By Otto Butz, Visiting Research Scholar, Center of International Studies, Princeton University

The Role of the Military in American Foreign Policy
By Burton M. Sapin, Research Assistant, Foreign Policy Analysis Project, Princeton University and Richard C. Snyder, Associate Professor of Politics, Princeton University

Democratic Rights Versus Communist Activity
By Thomas I. Cook, Professor of Political Science, The Johns Hopkins University

The Social Background of Political Decision-Makers
By Donald R. Matthews, Assistant Professor of Government, Smith College

Readings in Game Theory and Political Behavior
By Martin Shubik, Research Associate, Economic Analysis Project, Princeton University

Fall, 1954

The American Vice-Presidency: New Look
By Irving G. Williams, Associate Professor and Chairman, Departments of History and Social Studies, St. John's University

Contemporary International Law: A Balance Sheet
By Quincy Wright, Professor of Political Science, University of Chicago

Law as a Political Instrument
By Victor G. Rosenblum, Assistant Professor of Political Science, University of California, Berkeley

The Political Fate of the Non-Communist Left in Postwar France
By E. Drexel Godfrey, Jr., Assistant Professor of Political Science, Williams College

The Political Process: Executive Bureau—Congressional Committee Relations
By J. Leiper Freeman, Assistant Professor and Research Associate, Graduate School of Education, Harvard University

Agriculture and Politics: A Study in Power
By Robert Engler, Professor of Political Science, Sarah Lawrence College

Studies in Scope and Methods

The Study of Public Administration
By Dwight Waldo, Professor of Political Science, University of California, Berkeley

The Study of Political Theory
By Thomas P. Jenkin, Professor of Political Science and Chairman of the Department, University of California, Los Angeles

The Study of Comparative Government
By Roy C. Macridis, Associate Professor of Political Science, Northwestern University

Problems of Analyzing and Predicting Soviet Behavior
By John S. Reshetar, Jr., Lecturer in Politics, Princeton University

You may enter your subscription for the series now so that you will be sure to receive on approval each study as soon as it is published. The studies will be priced at no more than $1.00. Address COLLEGE DEPARTMENT, Doubleday & Company, Inc., 575 Madison Avenue, New York 22, N.Y.

Preface

We have set for ourselves some rather modest purposes in this short study. Despite the wide recognition among political scientists, government officials, and knowledgeable laymen that the expanded role of the military in American foreign policy has raised both actual and potential difficulties, considerable time has passed without any attempt at a general analysis. Much of the writing—and there has been a substantial amount—has been directed at particular aspects of military participation in policy-making. A good part of it has been polemical: it has argued the case for and against the danger of military dominance. This has been useful, especially in alerting the public to undesirable conditions, but has not provided a systematic presentation of the crucial factors involved.

We have attempted, first, to sketch in the background of the new role of the military—some of the reasons for it and some of the consequences of the interdependence of foreign policy and military policy which are felt by civilian and military officials alike. Second, we have outlined the dimensions of the new role by describing and interpreting the nature of military participation as best we could in the light of existing knowledge. Having enumerated the major functions, situations, and relationships in which the military are involved, we have gone on to our third purpose, the formulation of the central problem: an appropriate role for the military in foreign policy, given democratic values and the necessity for military advice and competence in the preservation of national security. In so doing, we have tried to separate, in terms of our analysis, real from spurious threats to civilian supremacy. Finally, we have suggested certain conditions under which we feel the proper contribution of the military could be preserved without subverting the principle of civilian supremacy and other values.

The subject matter of this book is controversial and will continue to be so. Though attempting to be dispassionate in our analysis we have not intended to carry water on both shoulders with respect to the existence of an important problem. We are convinced that there is a critical need for further study and discussion, and also that unless the civilian-military relationship in foreign-policy formation is clearly understood, real dangers may emerge. On the other hand, we are equally certain that it is essential for arguments concerning the extent of the threat to civilian supremacy, and solutions to the problem of appropriate military participation, to be undergirded with solid analysis which goes beyond epithet and value judgments. We have been able to do no more than indicate some of the directions such analysis might take. Eventually, monographs will be written on matters to which only a paragraph or two could be devoted here. The large-scale research being currently financed by the Carnegie Corporation, the Rockefeller Foundation, and the Twentieth Century Fund at Princeton, Columbia, and Dartmouth indicates increasing recognition of the need for concentrated scholarly effort.

Meanwhile it is hoped that the present synthesis will partially fill an obvious gap in the literature. The footnotes and the bibliographical suggestions should together provide the reader with a thorough, authoritative survey of existing sources and writings which deal with the role of the military in foreign policy.

Our acknowledgments and intellectual debts are numerous. We must thank the various members of the Princeton University community who have long labored in this area—Professors Harold Sprout, Edgar S. Furniss, Jr., Gordon Craig, Gordon Turner, and Dr. Harold Stein—for help knowingly and unknowingly given. We have drawn upon an unpublished memorandum by Lieutenant Colonel Marshall Sanders (USAF) and Lieutenant Colonel Richard Lee (USA) entitled *The Impact on American Foreign Policy of the Changing Relationships between Military and Civilian Groups*, which was prepared during their graduate work at Princeton under the supervision of Professors Snyder and Furniss. Many of the ideas briefly set forth in this study are derived from certain theoretical formulations being experimented with by the Foreign Policy Analysis Project at Princeton, of which we both are members. In that connection we owe a special debt of gratitude to our able colleague and friend, H. W. Bruck, the third member of the Project. One of the authors, Burton M. Sapin, was privileged to participate in a major study of the Japanese Peace Treaty undertaken by the Center of International Studies at Princeton University under the direction of Professor Frederick S. Dunn, Director of the Center. The result of this work was a doctoral dissertation on the role of the military in the formulation of the Japanese Peace Treaty. Finally, we wish to acknowledge the substantial contributions of the members of the Organizational Behavior Section at Princeton under the directorship of Professor Wilbert E. Moore.

Princeton, New Jersey   Burton M. Sapin
February 1, 1954   Richard C. Snyder

Contents

chapter one

The Expanded Role of the Military

One of the most striking and important developments in the United States since the end of the Second World War has been the greatly expanded activity and influence of the American Military Establishment in the life of the nation. The essential explanation for this lies, of course, in the emergence of the United States in the twentieth century as a great world power. The history of the last forty years—involvement in two world wars, then a cold war, intensified in turn by the outbreak of the Korean War in June 1950 and the substantial build-up of the American armed forces that followed—has meant increasing dependence on and attention to military strength, with a consequent increase in military activity, prestige, and influence.

This new role of the military has by no means gone unnoticed. Considerable interest and considerable concern have been expressed by many public officials and private citizens—outstanding scientists and educators, military critics, and students of government, as well as Congressmen, present and former high civilian officials both within and outside the Pentagon, and even high-ranking military officers themselves. A major recurring theme has been the danger of "creeping militarism," of the military "moving in," of the weakening or undermining of the American tradition of civilian supremacy.[1] Fear has been expressed that this increasing military influence may threaten democratic values and institutions and the maintenance of a flexible and broad-gauged civilian approach to foreign and domestic policy problems. The relief of General Douglas MacArthur by President Truman in April 1951 and the Senatorial hearings that followed dramatized some aspects of this question of the role of the military in the making of governmental policy and provoked considerable and widespread public discussion of the meaning of civil control over the military in a democratic society, though some of these issues did tend to get submerged or confused with the important differences on foreign policy between the General and the President.

Another fundamental concern has been the most economical and effective operation of the Defense Establishment with a view to obtaining the maximum security, of wise and well-ordered strategic planning, at minimum cost to the nation. One important manifestation of this concern has been the series of widely publicized major changes in the organizational structure of the armed forces that have taken place since 1947. In the last ten years the Pentagon has been examined by a number of official commissions and private study groups, and many of their recommendations have been put into effect. The process of study and adjustment is a continuing one, as evidenced by the fact that one of the reorganization plans presented to Congress by the Eisenhower Administration in 1953 dealt with the Military Establishment. The organization and activities of the Joint Chiefs of Staff have recently been subjected to criticism and suggestions for reform by such distinguished public figures as the outstanding scientific leader Vannevar Bush and the former Secretary of Defense, Robert Lovett. On the other hand, the "strengthening" of the Joint Chiefs has upon occasion brought forth expression of Congressional fears about the development of a Prussian-type general staff in this country.

Along with the attention to this problem from politicians and other public figures, an increasing interest in it has been shown by professional scholars and students in the field of political science. At the present time, some of the major research foundations in the country are supporting projects designed to study and evaluate the impact of the military on various aspects of American life and, more particularly, on national-policy-making. Such a development reflects the fact that while some recent books and articles have been devoted in full or in part to this problem, there is actually a paucity of useful, systematic, integrated studies.[2]

All in all, there can be little doubt but that the role of the American Military Establishment in the formulation and execution of national policy (as well as its wider impact on the society) represents an important contemporary political and social problem. It is also essentially a new problem, in part because traditional American values and institutions in the field of civil-military relations have never before been so severely challenged.

Traditional Civil-Military Relationships

It is not possible to spell out in detail the attitudes and interaction patterns that have, historically, characterized civil-military relations in the United States; but a brief comment is in order. The traditional civilian attitude toward the military has been one of suspicion and distrust, even positive dislike. The reasons for this are pretty obvious. First, there are the (oft-mentioned) experiences of the colonial period, marked by British employment of mercenary soldiers and the quartering of British troops in American homes without the consent of their owners. More generally, there are the all too many instances in the past, in the Old World and elsewhere, of military force used to install or support tyrannical governments. In the eyes of most Americans the actual values and attitudes of professional military men, or those ascribed to them, seemed inimical to freedom and democracy, to the cherished principles and institutions of the society. Thus it was neither safe nor wise to make the military forces too strong or to give military men wide powers and responsibilities.

That Americans have been to a certain extent ambivalent in this attitude is suggested by the fact that this nation has had its great military heroes. Career officers have been elected to the Presidency on six occasions. General Eisenhower is of course the most recent example. Furthermore, there has been less fear of the Navy than of the Army. This is probably accounted for in part by the comparatively small shore establishment required by a navy and also by the fact that navies have not traditionally been viewed as instruments of domestic political tyranny. There is the further point that the United States had important trade and maritime relations with other nations before it became so heavily involved in international politics that major diplomatic and military commitments became necessary.

Distrust and Dislike of the Military

The traditional distrust and dislike of the military was reflected in a number of ways. It is to be found in various articles and clauses of the Constitution. One of the enumerated powers and duties of the President is that he "shall be Commander-in-Chief of the Army and Navy of the United States, and of the Militia of the several States, when called into the actual service of the United States." Thus the Constitution in effect provides for a civilian chief of the armed forces. Only Congress can declare war, and it must raise and support the land and naval forces as well as provide for their organization, procedures, and regulations. At the same time Congressional appropriation powers are explicitly limited by the proviso that no appropriation of money for these purposes be for a longer period than two years. In actual practice Congress votes on the military budget yearly. The Constitution also lays considerable stress on the state militia and at the same time separates them from the national forces, reserving to the states the appointment of officers and the actual training of these troops, according to rules prescribed by Congress. In a larger sense, the Constitution is designed to prevent any one group or branch of the government from gaining too much power, from being in a position to dominate the whole governmental structure.

The fears of the military and of centralized governmental power reflected in the Constitution did not disappear with its ratification. For the most part the American Army was kept at minimum strength. In time of crisis and war, considerable reliance was placed on the state militia and on volunteer forces. There was no formal machinery through which the advice of high-ranking military officers on problems of national security and foreign policy could be made regularly available to civilian leaders in the executive branch. Nor was there any tradition of consultation with them on these problems. Indeed, it might be argued that for a considerable period in American history there was no clear conception of the possible ways in which military strength and military strategy might contribute to the effective conduct of foreign relations. In the past the American military usually entered into the field of foreign relations only when the country had become involved in a war or when military force was required for peacetime sanctions. At this point the military effort sometimes became the major foreign-policy technique of the nation; but once order was restored, the military returned to their isolation.

Social Isolation of the Military

Perhaps the most important fact about the traditional situation of the military vis-à-vis the civilians of the society was that they tended to be somewhat insulated from them. Military personnel, often at isolated posts and bases, were outside the main currents of American life. This was bound to have some impact on their view of the world and, more particularly, on their ability to consider nonmilitary factors in their planning, training, and operations. Naturally there was a tendency for the military to reciprocate civilian dislike, to resent poor pay, poor treatment, and the meager resources put at their disposal. This was compounded by a certain contempt for a civilian society oriented to material comfort and success to the exclusion of concern for the nation's security. It is not surprising that this attitude should have led many officers to see themselves as the main guardians of the nation and to distrust civilian abilities and views with respect to national defense.

The consequences of these civilian and military attitudes in national policy and in the size, training, equipment, and readiness of the armed forces did not prove disastrous or threatening to the American nation for a long time. Well into the twentieth century a number of favorable conditions prevailed. There were, first of all, the weak neighbors to the north and south. East and west were the great, wide oceans. Furthermore, as is well known, the United States was a prime beneficiary of *Pax Britannica* and a British Navy that dominated the world's sea lanes. Finally, the United States, with a continent to conquer and amid the aforementioned weak neighbors, was not for the most part subject to the kind of foreign involvements that might precipitate a major conflict with any of the great world powers.

This general sketch of traditional civil-military relations in the United States is suggestive only. But broadly the picture is one of civilian distrust of military force and "the military mind," distrust embodied in the laws and customs of the land; of reciprocated military resentment and some contempt for the civilians of the society; and of a narrowly trained, professional military elite somewhat insulated from the main currents of the society. To repeat, all of this had no disastrous consequences because of the peculiar immunity from international politics enjoyed by the country. These characterizations serve to accent the basic and deep-seated nature of the contemporary concern about a "proper" role for the military in the making of foreign and domestic policy, and also provide an impressive contrast with present-day attitudes, inclinations, and activities in the same area.[3]

Recent Changes in the Role of the Military

The contrast provided by the contemporary situation is all the more striking when it is remembered that much, probably the greater part, of what is about to be described represents a development of the last decade.

The impact of the American Military Establishment and its professional officer personnel on the government and the nation in recent years has been substantial and nearly all-encompassing. To say this is by no means to suggest or imply that the military have for all practical purposes taken over the direction of the nation, but simply to recognize that there are few areas of national life that have not been affected to some extent by their manifold activities. It is a far cry from their isolation and insulation of earlier days.

Impact on the Economy

Many books testify to the significant—some would say dominant—role of the armed forces in the mobilization and direction of the American economy during World War II. Clearly, the military budget has come to be an important factor in the American economy in the last fifteen years. Its size and character have important consequences for the allocation of limited resources of labor, capital, and raw materials. The procurement policies of the military departments may in effect make or break certain businesses. The power that rests with some of these officers and their civilian superiors in the Pentagon may perhaps be most simply indicated by pointing out that the Military Establishment has at its disposal funds and resources far outstripping those of the largest industrial corporations of the nation.

These funds and resources make the military agencies probably the largest single supporter of scientific research in the country today. Such research includes research in the social as well as in the physical sciences, pure as well as applied research. During the Second World War the Manhattan District Project, which did the work on the atomic bomb, was directed by the War Department. Under the Atomic Energy Act of 1946, the program was turned over to a five-man civilian commission. The substantial support given to scientific research by the military has, of course, raised serious questions as to the compatibility of military security requirements and military attitudes toward secrecy and security with the free and open atmosphere traditionally associated with scientific endeavors.

Impact on Education

A closely related development is the increasing activity of the armed services in the field of education. The ROTC program, begun during the First World War, has since expanded considerably and is now a familiar feature of the curriculum of many American colleges and universities. During the Second World War there were military-training units of various kinds at a great majority of American colleges. It is likely that many of these schools could not have survived without the financial aid provided by such units. One interesting trend since the war has been the dispatching of officers to various universities for advanced training in a considerable number of fields: public administration, international politics, foreign languages and cultures, and other social studies, as well as work in electronics, rocket propulsion, and other fields of physical science. There are even a number of Ph.D.'s wearing colonel's insignia to be found in the armed forces today.

The most obvious and fundamental educational impact of the Military Establishment lies in the fact that each year several hundred thousand men come under its control and discipline for a two-year period of duty, to be trained (sometimes provided with new and worthwhile skills), disciplined, and then made part of its complex structure of activities and operations either at home or abroad. If some sort of program of universal military training is ever instituted, it would obviously increase this aspect of the military's educational impact. In fact, doubts about the desirability of intensifying this kind of influence which might threaten the democratic values and attitudes of the nation's youth seem to underlie some of the strenuous opposition to a UMT program.

Selection for Nonmilitary Positions

So far, the instances of military activity and influence pointed to stem directly from the assigned tasks and responsibilities of the armed forces. However, one of the more noteworthy aspects of this "new" role of the military is the extent to which high-ranking military officers have moved into important private and governmental positions outside the Military Establishment. Retired generals and admirals have become top executives of large industrial corporations. Furthermore, military men have moved into high diplomatic and political posts. For example, General Eisenhower's wartime Chief of Staff, General W. Bedell Smith, was for several years Ambassador to Moscow, then headed the Central Intelligence Agency, and in the new Eisenhower Administration became Undersecretary of State. General George C. Marshall has had an even more distinguished postwar career—Secretary of State from 1947 to 1949, Secretary of Defense in 1950–1951, and 1953 the first military man ever to receive the Nobel Peace Prize. There are other examples. Admiral Alan Kirk was Ambassador to Belgium and then to the Soviet Union. Before his appointment as Chairman of the Joint Chiefs of Staff, General Omar Bradley served as head of the Veterans' Administration.

There can be no doubt that military officers have emerged as an important leadership group in contemporary American society. They are as a whole highly respected and greatly admired. Their views on a wide range of subjects are listened to with considerable attention and respect. They have become popular guest speakers at business luncheons and other social functions. Perhaps inevitably, some of them have entered or been forced into the arena of partisan politics and have become active spokesmen for particular policies or active supporters of one of the major political parties.

Involvement in Major Foreign-Policy Developments

To get some sense of the impact of the Military Establishment, military officers, military strength, and military considerations on the formulation and execution of American foreign policies and programs, one need go no further than the daily newspaper. The European Defense Community, NATO, military and economic aid to the French Union forces in Indo-China, the A-bomb, the H-bomb, guided missiles, the Strategic Air Command, the Korean War, air and naval bases in Spain, the military-assistance program for Western Europe—these are among the most important problems and foci of attention for American policy-makers and the American public. And the names of outstanding military figures indicate some of the major issues and landmarks in postwar United States policy—Eisenhower, Marshall, MacArthur, Bradley, now joined perhaps by Admiral Radford, General Gruenther, and General Ridgway. But because analyzing the role of the military in American foreign policy is, after all, the main purpose of this essay, nothing more need be said at this point. The new situation of the military is in sharp contrast to the traditional one, and has brought with it a number of serious problems and issues for the American nation.

Basic Reasons for These Changes

A brief answer to the question posed in this section is that the international situation of the United States has undergone a revolutionary change in recent years. However, some of the major features of the new position of the United States and their implications, both for national security and for the Defense Establishment, are worth pointing out in greater detail.

The Revolution in American Foreign Relations

Throughout most of the nineteenth century American relations with other nations were, roughly speaking, of secondary importance to matters of domestic politics and development. For reasons already noted, there was little danger of direct foreign attack. The present situation is obviously quite different. Relations with other nations are by all odds the primary consideration and focus of attention, both within the governmental structure and outside it. The essential reason for this is rather simple: the very survival of the nation is at stake in these relations. The United States is faced today with hostile nations capable not only of inflicting tremendous loss of life and material resources in war but even of defeating it, and perhaps in either case destroying the fabric of its fundamental values and institutions. Scientific and technological advances have made war in the middle of the twentieth century unbelievably destructive, and furthermore have made possible the application of these destructive techniques to almost any point on the globe. Such "all-out" war is a continuing and ever-present possibility, and there is no guarantee that its coming would be preceded by any warning or that there would be any safety period for undisturbed mobilization once it began.

This last fact is of some significance, since a further consequence of scientific and technological advances is that war and preparations for war have become almost incomprehensibly complex and expensive. As has been said so many times, a modern war machine cannot be created overnight. This means that given the present danger, a great deal of planning is necessary, requiring detailed preparation for a series of political, economic, and military contingencies. At the stage of all-out war, a full mobilization of national wealth, resources, and population would be necessary. Presumably another world war would bring home the nature of total war to the American nation with much greater severity than did World War II.

Another factor to be noted is the great number and variety of skills needed to meet the demands of modern war. Many of these skills demand considerable training and experience. For the most part they too cannot be developed overnight. As far as the armed forces themselves are concerned, the day is long since past when the hastily mobilized citizen-soldier can take his place on the battle line alongside his professional compatriot, or when the necessary military goods can be produced from scratch in a matter of weeks or months.

It thus seems clear that the international environment with which the United States must presently cope demands the maintenance of considerable military strength-in-being (including appropriate productive resources and trained personnel). Such "readiness potential" (to use Hanson Baldwin's phrase) will be sufficient, it is hoped, to deter possible enemies, but if not, it is essential that instantaneous and effective counteraction be forthcoming in case of attack. While there may be strong disagreement regarding the exact military strength-in-being that would be most conducive to the security of the nation, there is little disagreement that a substantial permanent military establishment is unavoidable, given the present state of the world.

In sum, the fundamental safety of the nation is at stake and must presumably be a prime consideration in American relations with other nations. There are, surely, important differences in the ways in which national security can be defined. There are likewise different views as to the most appropriate or effective means of achieving it. Such divergences are likely to lead to the recommendation of different policies and programs. However, few would be inclined to deny the importance of military strength and the use, or threat of use, of military force in the relations of the United States with other nations. They are not the only factors, and, many would argue, not even the most significant factors in the present situation; but military tools and techniques are certainly fundamental to the conduct of diplomacy by the United States at present.

Present Responsibilities of the Military Establishment

In general, the foregoing reflections show that the American Defense Establishment must be prepared to meet, and in an eventual sense deal successfully with, a number of possible contingencies involving the use of United States armed forces. This must be done by the military disposing of what are limited or scarce resources—that is, it is simply not possible to be fully prepared to meet all possible contingencies successfully. Furthermore, because of differing estimates of the danger and the impact of important nonmilitary pressures and problems, the military are not even able to command all the resources which might be desirable under ideal circumstances. Operating within the framework of certain major national objectives in the international sphere and of certain implementing national policies and programs, and on the basis of certain assumptions about the capabilities and the intentions of other nations, both friends and potential enemies, the military are responsible (1) for continuing strategic planning designed to prepare for various contingencies, and (2) in terms of these plans and assumptions, for training, equipping, and appropriately disposing national forces that will be capable of dealing successfully with those threats to the security of the nation involving the application of force of arms by other nations. Plainly, the burdens that the military carry today are heavy, not to say staggering.

They are further complicated by the fact that besides maintaining a substantial military force of its own, the United States is engaged in building up the armed strength of some of the nations allied with it. For the military this means additional responsibilities. There are questions of national capabilities and intentions, assessments of the military potentialities of the countries being aided, and decisions as to what types of training and equipment would be most useful for them, and then whether such matériel is available in the necessary quantities. Such programs mean sending American military missions to the countries involved, for purposes of assessment and negotiation regarding their military needs and of training their forces in the use of the equipment sent.

A further series of problems arises because military preparation involves having forces not only on hand but also in positions from which they can most economically and most effectively be sent into action. In the present state of the world, this seems to require stationing considerable American forces at overseas bases, which in most cases must be in the metropolitan territory or colonial possessions of other sovereign nations. These bases in turn involve diplomatic negotiations establishing the detailed conditions under which the American forces are to operate, and a great number of small and large problems connected with the relations between the American troops and their foreign "hosts."

This account has so far failed to mention the two most immediately significant operations of the military in the last few years—the Korean War and the international army of the North Atlantic Treaty Organization (NATO). In the Korean struggle an important segment of American military strength was engaged in a "limited war" for a period of three years. Perhaps more important, in terms of major consequences and implications for foreign policy, is the fact that American generals commanded an international army fighting, for the first time in history, under the banner of an international organization comprising most of the nations of the world. These American-directed military operations did have important foreign-policy implications, some of which will be suggested below.

Since the beginning of 1951, forces of the North Atlantic Treaty countries in Western Europe have been commanded by a succession of three American generals in their appointed role as SACEUR (Supreme Allied Commander, Europe). In contrast to the Korean operation, which was predominantly American-run and American-staffed, the Supreme Headquarters near Paris has a large contingent of non-American officers. European generals and admirals occupy a great many of the top command positions. NATO is an international political organization with an international secretariat supporting it (its present Secretary-

General is the retired British general Lord Ismay) and also an international army with an appropriate central Headquarters, which is constantly engaged in what must be called *international* military planning.

The American Military Establishment has also carried out other important tasks assigned to it, notably the occupation and direction of defeated enemy countries for a considerable period after the end of World War II; but the tasks already enumerated should make unmistakably clear the many and complex ways in which military policies and military activities are closely tied to and intermixed with American foreign policies and programs.

Interdependence of Foreign Policy and Military Policy

Clearly the greatly increased role of the military can be explained in good part by the crucial importance of the military equation in international politics. It is also clear that this dependence of American foreign policy on military strength has major consequences for the military as well as for the makers of foreign policy. As far as national security is concerned, military and nonmilitary factors are so closely interrelated that they may be thought of as inseparable aspects of particular problems and situations.[4]

Nature and Consequences of Interdependence

Military strength is only one of the prerequisites of national security, and the use of military force or pressure is only one of a variety of techniques available to the policy-maker. For the most part, military power is simply the means to various ends—survival, prevention of aggression, and so on. Essentially the military are most concerned with *how* certain foreign policies are to be carried out and *how* military threats are to be met. They are concerned with *what* policies only to the extent that the question of military feasibility arises. Military policy must be determined within a general framework of foreign policy. Such a framework may be called, to use Edward Mead Earle's concept, "grand strategy"—an effective integration of the nation's policies and armaments. Two things seem to be implied by this line of argument: first, in a fundamental sense, foreign policy is superior to military policy in that military considerations do not determine what national objectives are appropriate, although the latter may be limited by available military means; second, because successful action depends on an effective combination of ends and means, foreign policy and military policy must be coordinated. Hence a general framework of foreign policy must exist as a guide to the effective use of military techniques, *and* military policies must not become ends in themselves.

One of the criticisms made of American policy during World War II was that it was preoccupied with gaining quick and complete military victory and thus gave less consideration than was wise to political problems and objectives of longer range. In other words, military operations were apparently conducted without any larger framework of political purposes and objectives to guide them. This may or may not be a valid criticism in this case, but the general point it makes seems to be well taken. A more recent example is provided by the Korean War. Here many people, including Generals Douglas MacArthur and James Van Fleet and some members of Congress, have argued that it was necessary to push on to complete military victory in 'Korea; otherwise, American policy there could be regarded as a failure. The point apparently ignored by these people is that the military operations, and the great destruction and loss of life they entailed, only made sense in terms of a set of larger political objectives, and that the nature and extent of the military operations conducted must necessarily be determined in the light of these objectives and not vice versa.

The larger foreign-policy framework on which military policy should be based must also include a series of assumptions about the intentions and the strength of other nations. One of the fundamental concerns of the United States today relates to the foreign-policy intentions of the Soviet Union. Considerable money and effort are now being expended, in both overt and covert intelligence operations, to gain accurate information on which sound estimates can be based. Another pertinent question with regard to the Soviet Union is the nature of its internal social and political stability and what factors work either to disturb or to strengthen it. But it is not only the Soviet Union and the countries in its orbit that concern the United States. This framework of objectives and assumptions presumably includes also forecasts about future political stability in France, the viability of the Japanese economy, and the possibility of resurgent Nazism in West Germany, among many other matters.

Given this dependence of military policy on American grand strategy, what are some of the consequences for the military? Obviously, changes in foreign-policy objectives or programs may call for important revisions in military strategic thinking or in military estimates of manpower and matériel needs. Two recent examples of this are the involvement in Korea and the decision to station large numbers of American troops in Europe as part of the NATO army. Apparently the invasion of South Korea by the North Koreans produced some changes in American assumptions about the immediacy of the threat of total war, which accounted at least in part for the quick build-up in American military strength after June 1950.

Another obvious consequence for the military of the close relation of foreign and military policy is that a great many of the problems and situations in relation to which their plans must be made pose questions which lie far outside the traditional area of military expertise. Thus to a considerable extent they are dependent on civilian skills, information, and knowledge in a number of areas.

The essential point of this discussion seems undeniable: the Military Establishment's programs and policies with respect to armament development, force levels, overseas bases, and allocation of resources among the three Services will all depend significantly on the total foreign-policy program and commitments of the nation. As already noted, the reverse is also true: American foreign-policy decisions must be evaluated in the light of military factors—mobilized and potential power, plans and strategies, changing weapons systems, and assessment of risks and contingencies. In the words of the National Security Act of 1947, it is necessary "to assess and appraise the objectives, commitments, and risks of the United States in relation to our actual and potential military power."[5] Arthur Schlesinger, Jr., in a recent article analyzing the substantial cuts in the military budget made by the Eisenhower Administration in 1953, makes the following interesting observation:

It is now evident that military power becomes the master of foreign policy not when there is too much of it but when there is too little. It is the absence or lopsidedness of armed strength that allows the military situation to run foreign affairs. When our military policy is inadequate to meet a variety of crises, our foreign policy must become constrained, rigid, and inflexible. Balanced and ample military power is consequently the price we must pay for freedom of national action.[6]

This has apparently been the view of American policy-makers in recent years, since much of their effort has been designed to build up the military strength of the United States and nations allied to or friendly with it. The basic assumption underlying this approach was that one vital and necessary way of deterring the Soviet Union from certain courses of action was to build up significant military strength among the nations of the "free world." In turn, one way to build up the courage and the possibility of freer and more flexible action on the part of these nations outside the Communist orbit was to give them the hope and the material means of national survival through self-defense. Given a "situation of strength" among the nations outside the Soviet world, it might be possible to negotiate gradually and slowly some sort of *modus vivendi* between these two groups of nations. Thus American foreign policy since 1947 has been marked by such politico-military policies and programs as the Truman Doctrine of aid to Greece and Turkey, the North Atlantic Treaty and the international army that has been established under its aegis, the military-assistance programs for Western Europe and such nations as Yugoslavia and Iran, the three Pacific security treaties involving the Philippines, Japan, Australia, and New Zealand, the substantial program of military and economic aid to the French Union states of Indo-China, and the proposed and much-emphasized European Defense Community under which German troops would be brought into the defense of Western Europe.

Security Planning and the Time Factor

The international situation has tended to be in continual rapid change in recent years. This means that significant developments must if possible be anticipated, and necessary changes made in assumptions and programs. In such a setting, time assumptions and time perspectives are of considerable importance for the military as well as for others. Military planning must be based on assumptions about *when* certain situations are likely to become threatening, *when* a major enemy is going to be able to mount a devastating atomic air attack on the United States, *when* Japan is going to be able to defend itself without the need of American forces, and so on. These are obviously difficult questions, but reasonable estimates with regard to them would seem to be of utmost importance for the military.

Since the subject, though an important one, is usually ignored, it may be useful to suggest ways in which time factors affect the Pentagon's planning and the carrying out of its duties. For one thing, the present rapid rate of obsolescence of weapons and weapons systems produces a host of difficulties and dilemmas. In allocating the limited resources put at their disposal, the military must decide how many weapons of what quality are to be ready *when.* If they overestimate the immediacy of the danger of hostilities and put their then-best weapons into mass production, they are in all likelihood going to accumulate great quantities of matériel that will be obsolete when hostilities actually do arrive. On the other hand, it does take considerable time to get a modern airplane or tank from the designer's drawing board into full-scale production, and further time to equip forces and train them in the use of the new equipment. There is also the matter of needing time to iron out the difficulties that sometimes arise in the field with even the most carefully designed and tested weapons. Operating thus with the most reliable assumptions available about the immediacy and urgency of possible military threats to the nation, the military must draw some kind of balance between the necessity of having currently mobilized forces appropriately equipped and keeping on hand stockpiles of weapons and ammunition to meet possible short-run contingencies, while at the same time maintaining research and engineering activities and readily available though currently unused productive facilities, to assure continuing production of the best available weapons in the quantities needed at the time needed. An illustration of this problem is provided by a controversy in early 1952 over a reported shortage of ammunition among American forces in Korea. Testimony before a Senate investigating subcommittee indicated that while the shortage could probably be blamed in part on inefficient procurement procedures in the Army Department, it was in good part explained by an assumption about when the Korean War would end that turned out, with hindsight wisdom, to be optimistic.[7] Probably some of the critics who deplored the "shortage" would have taken the Army to task for maintaining overlarge ammunition inventories if the Joint Chiefs of Staff had operated on the assumption of a longer war and the truce had come two years sooner than it did.

The need for explicit and reliable time assumptions and perspectives is further accented by the complicated and sometimes erratic budgetary process that characterizes the United States Government. The military requests, once agreed upon within the Defense Establishment (and this is not likely to be easy), must go through several further stages of clearance and approval within the executive branch. Once they have cleared these hurdles, they must pass through the several stages of Congressional inspection and scrutiny. It is not surprising, then, that officers and officials in the Pentagon are likely to be working on budget requests for a fiscal year that is twelve or even eighteen months away. This further emphasizes the importance of their assumptions, and at the same time the possibility that the time interval between budget planning and Congressional voting of appropriations may produce developments that make these assumptions invalid. There is another factor to be mentioned—what Arthur Macmahon calls the "inertia of rest and motion" in the budgetary process; that is, the difficulty of making important changes very quickly, whether raising goals suddenly and substantially and getting an expanded program rolling, or lowering goals and objectives if this seems desirable.[8] Finally, as has been suggested, a considerable period of time—sometimes measured in years—must usually elapse between the voting of the appropriation by Congress and the actual delivery of the "hardware" to the Military Establishment.

Global Political Judgments

A related aspect of the military's problem, briefly alluded to above, deserves attention. National military strategy and planning involve some awareness and interpretation of a global situation in which there are a considerable number of problems and possibilities of widely varying clarity and seriousness. Given the limitations on resources, the question of priorities and risks arises. Various possible assumptions, expectations, and contingencies must be balanced with a view to employing these resources in a reasonably effective way. In the present international situation of the United States, risks cannot be avoided, they can only be minimized. In a period of severe and continuing military danger, this balancing is by no means an enviable task. It makes apparently exaggerated and oversized military budget requests understandable, if not necessarily to be accepted unquestioningly. As a final point, it is difficult to imagine the military arriving at a judicious and defensible balance of risks, costs, and priorities in their plans and programs unless these rested on the kind of larger grand strategy of American foreign policy suggested above.

If it is necessary to emphasize confusion and complexity further, it might be suggested that there is often not complete agreement on the nature of the guiding policy framework. For example, there may be important disagreements between military and civilian officials, or even within each group, as to Soviet military capabilities, or equally important, Soviet intentions. There may also be disagreement on what policies and programs are most likely to achieve basic American purposes and objectives. How does one weigh the military advantages of United States air and naval bases in Spain against the political, moral, and psychological disadvantages that some critics of this agreement profess to see? In any case, it would seem to be important for all concerned to accept the need for a grand strategy and to be somewhat self-conscious about their own assumptions, preferences, and priorities, as well as the policy and program consequences that appear to follow from them.

Living with Civilian Decisions

In the American democratic system the final decisions as to the balance to be drawn in military planning and military spending, the costs to be borne, and the risks to be taken lie with the politically responsible civilian leaders of the nation —the President, the civilian department heads of the Defense Establishment, and the Congress. Within his own sphere, Defense Secretary Charles E. Wilson made clear his own acceptance of this view and the responsibilities entailed in it in his decisions on Military Establishment budgets for the fiscal years 1953–54 and 1954–55. The professional officers of the armed forces must of course accept these decisions and the risks they involve, even though from their own viewpoint the risks may seem excessive. While the military did not openly oppose the "New Look," their interpretation of the budget reductions betrayed certain anxieties and differed from that of their civilian colleagues.

As was noted above, the military must also "live with" the foreign-policy decisions made by the nation's civilian leaders and the important military consequences that they have often had in recent years. Whether or not they agreed to the decisions or were in favor of them, and whether or not the decisions were made with careful attention to possible military consequences, the military must try to deal with those consequences involving military strength or the application of military force. The Korean War provides some striking illustrations of this point. In fact the very decision to intervene when South Korea was invaded was apparently made against the military advice of the Joint Chiefs of Staff, though it was regarded as justifiable on political grounds as upholding the idea of collective security and refusing to let an aggressor nation pursue its course without interference or punishment. There had been an earlier military decision that South Korea was of little strategic importance and that there was little need or hope of defending it if war came. However, the decision was made to intervene, and the consequences that followed for the Military Establishment by way of activities and responsibilities are too widespread and complicated, and too well known, to be discussed here. A later foreign-policy decision on Korea that had important implications for military strategy and operations was the one that limited the war to Korea itself and prevented extension of operations to Manchuria and the coast of Communist China. In this case, the decision was also supported by most military officers for so-called "purely military" reasons.

Nonmilitary Effects of Military Operations

The Military Establishment has had important responsibilities in carrying out many foreign-policy decisions and programs. Inevitably military decisions and actions have resulted that bring important *nonmilitary* consequences for America's relations with other nations. The Korean War again provides some interesting illustrations. Some of the seemingly tactical military decisions were actually fraught with important political implications. Without attempting to criticize or blame the generals involved (for the responsibility could lie with weak civilian leadership as well as with military indiscretion or lack of good judgment) one can point to the decision to cross the 38th Parallel into North Korea, the later decision to push up to the Yalu River and the Manchurian border of Communist China, and in June 1952 General Mark Clark's order for a bombing raid on North Korean power plants along the Yalu River while truce negotiations were in progress with the Communist forces. (The French and British Governments immediately criticized this raid as an ill-considered gesture which might have unfortunate political consequences.) Some observers are inclined to argue that the crossing of the 38th Parallel, followed by the drive of the United Nations forces deep into North Korea, may have provided the stimulus for the entry of Communist China into the Korean War. Certainly if this was a possible consequence of these particular military decisions, then they immediately take on much more than tactical military significance and should have been treated accordingly.

General Douglas MacArthur's removal from the United Nations command in Korea by President Truman was designed to ensure that no further military decisions would be taken which might threaten the larger political objectives of the United States and the United Nations, once it became clear that the General was in strong disagreement with these objectives.

The truce negotiations in Korea provide another example of a seemingly narrow military situation that in fact has or develops important political and diplomatic overtones and implications. Certainly the Communist negotiators viewed them in this light from the very start; and while American policy-makers may not have completely understood this at first, they apparently soon accepted the fact. Though the United Nations representatives throughout the long negotiations were career military officers, they seem to have been supplied with State Department advice and instructions. In April 1953, when the negotiations seemed to be coming to a head, Robert D. Murphy, then retiring United States Ambassador to Japan (and now a high official in the State Department) was appointed special political adviser to General Clark, the United Nations Supreme Commander, to assist him in dealing with the truce situation. The question of the repatriation of prisoners of war, on which the two sides were so long deadlocked, represented nothing more or less than a basic difference in human values between the Communist and United Nations sides.

The whole NATO operation represents an ambitious and highly complicated politico-military venture. As many observers have noted, the role of the American general who is Supreme Commander has important political and diplomatic aspects. In fact, General Eisenhower was the choice of the European NATO nations to be the first SACEUR in large part because it was felt that he could provide the leadership necessary to achieve a much-needed unity and vigor of action. He and his successors have spent a great deal of their time in conferences and discussions with the political leaders of Western Europe. Another interesting illustration of the impact of military considerations and actions upon larger political relationships is provided by the reluctance of the United States Navy to allow its forces to be under the command of foreign admirals if United States forces made up the bulk of the fleet in question. With regard to both the Atlantic and the Mediterranean naval commands of NATO, this United States Navy position ran into the equally stubborn pride and sensibilities of Sir Winston Churchill and Great Britain's Royal Navy. Obviously, these were not major difficulties or crises, but they nevertheless indicate how military responsibilities that seem simple and clear-cut may have their larger diplomatic consequences. Of course, the size of the American forces abroad and the extent and nature of military assistance granted and sent are so clearly part of a larger policy that the major decisions concerning them are made by the top civilian leaders of the nation.

Mass-Destruction Weapons and Foreign Policy

There is one further aspect of the military impact on foreign policy which should be stressed. It is the great influence on contemporary international politics of weapons development and comparative national advantages in weapons. Certainly nations have in the past paid considerable attention to military technology and have won or lost battles and perhaps even wars (though this is less likely) through the introduction of some startling innovation in military armament or tactics. However, in the age of the atomic and hydrogen bombs, intercontinental bombing planes, guided missiles, supersonic speeds, and complex electronic devices, the significant and far-reaching consequences of developments in weapons systems seem particularly impressive. Whatever one may say about other countries, there can be no doubt that the people and high officials of the United States have paid considerable attention to these developments and have apparently relied to a great extent on a lead in the field of mass-destruction devices as a bulwark of their foreign policy.

For some time after the end of the Second World War it was said by many that exclusive possession of the atomic bomb by the United States was the main deterrent to aggressive warfare by the Soviet Union. Whether this was a reliable inference about the behavior of the men in the Kremlin and whether it was the point of view actually held by the people responsible for American foreign policy or not, the limited war fought in Korea from 1950 on suggested that the atomic-bomb-carrying Strategic Air Command built up by the United States was an "all-out war" weapon of little or no use in the kind of struggle being waged in Korea. If the Communist world is capable of starting other such local wars— wars which could not justifiably be regarded as provocation for an all-out war (and this is at least questionable)—then the United States would obviously be restricting the deterrent force of its military posture and the range of its policy choices if it continued to depend too heavily on its air-atomic military armory to the exclusion of other weapons. In his article previously cited, Arthur Schlesinger, Jr., bluntly argues this point of view when he says:

> The strategic air-power theory commits us to maximum force or nothing. It gives us the choice between making faces at the enemy and blowing up the world. It offers no solution to the typical technique of Soviet aggression, which is not all-out war but a succession of frontier wars.[9]

This is, of course, an oversimplification of the problem, for the United States has since 1950 substantially strengthened the other elements in its armed forces —infantry divisions, tactical air units, the Navy, and so on. However, there is still considerable emphasis in the minds of the general public and in statements by public officials on the so-called unconventional weapons of mass destruction, the atomic and hydrogen bombs—"city-busters" rather than "block-busters"— and their importance in American foreign policy. This importance cannot be denied. Nor is it sensible to argue that the United States should abandon its research and production activities in the field of military applications of atomic fission and fusion. But the military significance of these weapons for the United States can be exaggerated; in any case, some of their less attractive political aspects and implications must be faced up to along with their much-advertised advantages.

The consequences of assuming that the United States would be able to maintain its monopoly of these weapons for a considerable period of time have already been demonstrated. Each time it has been announced or confirmed that the Soviet Union has ended American monopoly of one of these weapons—first of the atomic bomb and then of the hydrogen bomb—there has been considerable public uproar in the United States, and a number of statements have been issued by presumably responsible public officials that suggested deep fear and concern, not to say panic and hysteria. It must be assumed that this reaction was not shared at the highest levels in the United States Government, since if it were, it would suggest that foreign-policy thinking and planning depend in a way that seems highly undesirable on exclusive possession of a weapon, of one particular device within one particular set of tools and techniques—that is, the military—among the many available to the American statesman.

The Moral Issue

Reliance on these weapons raises other questions. For example, ever since pinpoint strategic bombing of military targets was replaced by saturation bombing of whole urban areas, observers have raised the moral issue of the deliberate and wanton destruction of "innocent and unprotected" civilians. To be sure, atomic bombing may not introduce a new moral issue, but only strikingly dramatize the original one. In any case, the moral issue should be faced up to and recognized for what it is. It might even have practical consequences at some point. For example, if some nation outside the Soviet bloc came up with a seemingly foolproof plan for the abolition of atomic warfare, a plan then accepted by the Soviet Union, the United States might be put in a most untenable position in the eyes of the world. This eventuality is unlikely, but not completely beyond the realm of possibility. Furthermore, it is all very well to talk glibly about the destruction of x number of Russian cities and y millions of Russian citizens on the first day of World War III; but what are likely to be the consequences for any larger political or moral purposes of the United States in such a war, and also for the rehabilitation and reconstruction that must follow when the war is won?

An essential clue in understanding the defeatism and neutralism that chacterized much of Western Europe, particularly before the coming into being of the NATO army in 1951, is that the Europeans looked forward with little enthusiasm to being overrun and then A-bombed before finally being liberated. Many of them had already suffered through such an experience in the Second World War. Accordingly, one of the reasons for building up European defense forces, sending large numbers of American ground forces and tactical air units to Great Britain and Western Europe, and continuing to maintain them there is to bolster European moral, to give the Europeans some sense that their own lands can be and will be defended from Russian attack. This morale factor would seem to be of sufficient importance to at least balance the view that an aggressor could be more effectively, and economically, intimidated by large strategic air forces based in the United States.

Capabilities and Vulnerabilities

Soviet possession of the atomic and hydrogen bombs raises a further series of questions of military technology that have important foreign-policy implications. First of all, it is important to know whether the Soviet Union has the ability—measured in terms of long-range planes (plus knowledge, skills, and trained men to operate them, probably less easily come by than the planes themselves) and perhaps other more devious delivery devices, like the oft-mentioned large trunk or suitcase—to deliver a large quantity of these bombs on American targets. If it is decided that the Russians do have or will have this ability at some date not too distant, then the question of air defense begins to assume considerable importance, for the maker of foreign policy as well as for the military man. In other words, if at some point in the future the Soviet Union and the United States will each have a substantial stockpile of these bombs and the ability to deliver impressive numbers of them on targets in the other nation, then the comparative ability of the two countries to defend themselves from these attacks becomes quite important. So does the question of comparative vulnerability of the two nations to this kind of attack. If it is true that the Russian industrial and transportation systems are less vulnerable to strategic air bombardment than those of the United States, this becomes a fact of considerable significance. In the last year, such distinguished scientists as J. Robert Oppenheimer and Lloyd V. Berkner, arguing along the lines suggested above, have urged the importance of building up the continental air defense of the United States.[10] Clearly if these views are at all accurate, a major advance in the techniques of antiaircraft defense by either side would be of considerable significance. This probably explains the attention and publicity given in recent months to the surface-to-air guided missiles now at an advanced stage of development in this country. Without a doubt, knowledge that the United States was very well protected from hostile air attack would be reassuring to those who make American foreign policy. On the other hand, knowledge that the Soviet Union had also developed impressive antiaircraft defenses would no doubt call for some important rethinking of American military policy and strategy, and inevitably of foreign policy as well.

In sum, weapons development in this country and abroad accounts for some important assumptions underlying the foreign policies pursued by the United States and the freedom of action retained by American policy-makers. Such technical military matters as the evaluation of different systems of weapons, the balance decided upon among the various kinds of weapons and forces (how many Air Force wings, how many guided-missile antiaircraft units, how many infantry and armored divisions), the absolute quantities of matériel available, and weapons development in other countries—all these become of considerable interest to the men responsible for making foreign policy, as well as to the officers and officials of the Defense Establishment. Equally important is the need to face up to all the implications—moral, political, and psychological as well as military—of these weapons and to the possible consequences of overdependence on any one weapon or set of weapons in terms of public attitudes, freedom of policy action, and the variety of possible contingencies that can be successfully dealt with. Without such an approach, weapons that seem to simplify the tasks of the policy-maker may actually serve in the end to complicate them.

It is assumed that the foregoing discussion of Military Establishment responsibilities in the middle of the twentieth century, and of the many and complex ways in which military policy and foreign policy are tied together and related to one another, has answered the question why the military have assumed an enhanced role in policy formation and execution. Foreign-policy decisions and programs clearly call for military advice, skills, knowledge, and resources. Equally, military planning and policies would seem to demand civilian advice and knowledge, as well as a clear and explicit framework of foreign-policy objectives and assumptions from which to proceed. In a recent report on the administration of foreign affairs, the staff of the Brookings Institution puts the matter this way:

> In the making of major decisions on foreign policy, the military voice should be heard even if it cannot always be heeded. For unless the military have an opportunity to advise, foreign policy commitments and military support for them may get dangerously out of balance. It is equally important that the civilian voice be heard in the formulation of strategic plans and of military policy generally. Otherwise military policies may be conceived without relation to the tasks set by national policy in which military strength may be required. There is a critical interdependence between foreign policy and military strength.[11]

Three Major Problems

The preceding discussion sets forth the circumstances under which the whole problem of what constitutes an appropriate role for the military in the formulation and execution of foreign policy has become vital for the American people. Actually, as already hinted, the problem is really a cluster of problems, that of civilian supremacy being most fundamental. In Chapters Four and Five these problems will be given further attention.

Civilian Supremacy

The central question can be put this way: *How can civilian supremacy be maintained in the policy-making relationships between civilian and military agencies and personnel, given the greatly expanded role of the military establishment and the impact foreign policy and military policy have on each other?*

Obvious questions that follow are What is the meaning of civilian supremacy or civil control? What are the institutional and other criteria for determining when it exists? Leaving more detailed analysis and discussion for a later point, let it be assumed that civilian supremacy obtains when major policy decisions are being made *effectively as well as formally* by the politically responsible civilian leaders of the nation, and the role of the military in national-policy-making is definitely limited and circumscribed. It can then be asked under what conditions such a situation will prevail, or possibly not prevail. Under what conditions is military participation possible, in making and executing foreign policy, without dominance of the process (or tendencies in that direction) by military values, objectives, information and intelligence, and judgments? In other words, how is it possible to profit by military advice and to use the specialized skills of the military without having foreign-policy decisions actually made by military officials, and without having foreign-policy problems defined solely or predominantly in military terms? It is generally conceded that the possibility of a military coup d'état or blatant usurpation of offices and powers not prescribed by law is remote. Indeed part of the difficulty is that the process of subverting civilian control—and as will be pointed out later, this can mean several different things—may go on quietly, unintentionally, and obscured from public view. It may not even be recognized. In order to cope with the problem effectively, it seems necessary that there be clear, agreed criteria for determining what constitutes military dominance, and recognition of the locations and situations in the decision-making structure of the National Government where challenges to civilian supremacy are most likely to arise.

The "Military Mind"

Given the developments noted briefly above, it is not surprising that there have emerged distrust and criticism of something called the military mind. Unfortunately this concept has not been systematically developed and clarified. However, the quotations that follow typify the reactions of some responsible and knowledgeable observers. Though not all experienced commentators would agree that the traits mentioned are predominant in most military personnel, the quotations indicate that serious critics do see sufficient evidence of disadvantageous qualities in military thinking to make it a matter of concern in studying contemporary civil-military relations.

Speaking of the military, Hanson Baldwin says: "Most of the men . . . are good public servants; many of them are exceptional. Collectively, however, they represent a pattern; they have in common the habit of command discipline and the mental outlook of military training—a tendency to apply in their thinking the yardstick of physical power. It is a pattern to be watched." Justice William O. Douglas argues that "the military mind is too narrow," by which he means that military education is too specialized and military techniques too limited in terms of foreign-policy problems. The military mind views world affairs solely in the perspective of preparedness for war and is opposed to public debate, dissent, and disagreement. Its response to social revolution is inappropriate. C. L. Sulzberger, after remarking that "there is popular suspicion of what is often referred to as the 'military mind'," goes on to state that it involves formal, rigid thinking and limited knowledge of social behavior generally. Arthur Schlesinger, Jr., includes among the qualities of the military mind the tendencies (a) to use military logic exclusively, (b) to see everything too clearly, and (c) to ignore ultimate values of a moral and spiritual sort. Referring to General Grant as President, John Marquand once wrote: "He was trained to be a soldier with a military mind and his deficiencies do not imply that a military mind necessarily unfits its owner to hold a high political office. Yet they indicate, perhaps, that the military mind does present its owner with specific handicaps which he must overcome in order to get on with the great mass of his fellow citizens, who have not been subjected to his disciplines and training. . . . All professional soldiers have similar attitudes and reactions unavoidably because they have the military mind." Finally, Fortune magazine has commented: "Our commanders have shown little talent for thinking beyond victorious force to the broad political situations"; and then gone on to set forth the rules of American military thinking: first, a set of alternatives so completely explored that only a course of action has to be chosen; second, the devising of sweeping plans which are to unfold inevitably step by step; third, the mobilization of overwhelming matériel and the mounting of huge operations; fourth, neat solutions, either-or propositions. These rules seem to flow naturally from American industrial potential, the successful application of massive force to detailed plans, and the desire to conserve human life. However, *Fortune* finds pragmatic opportunism lacking in strategic planning and also alleges that military intelligence suffers from quickly alternating attitudes of optimism and pessimism regarding enemy strength and intentions.[12]

These are quite typical interpretations of what is meant by the "military mind." The quotations seem to imply a combination of qualities which allegedly justify a severe indictment of the intellectual capabilities of the professional soldier. Apparently the disabilities apply not only to purely military functions but particularly to the foreign-policy contributions of the military. The disabilities are presumably due to training, tradition, experience, the nature of military techniques and objectives, and career membership in a highly bureaucratized organization. Concern over the nature of the military mind has increased because as military influence has increased, so naturally has the opportunity for this type of thinking to shape foreign policy. Triumph of the military point of view—if it includes these qualities—might in itself constitute a retreat from civilian supremacy.

The foregoing quotations stress certain attitudes, values, and perspectives deemed inappropriate for formulating and executing foreign policy. To summarize, the most serious criticisms of the military mind appear to be of alleged tendencies toward (a) rigidity in thought and problem analysis—the rejection of new ideas and reliance on tradition rather than lessons learned from recent experience; (b) inadequate weighing of nonmilitary factors in military problems, and inability to understand complex politico-military relationships; (c) an authoritarian approach to most social issues and situations, accompanied by disrespect for and disregard of civilian authority; (d) insulation from nonmilitary knowledge and anything beyond what is narrowly defined as militarily relevant; and (e) judgment of policy goals and techniques primarily in terms of military force and military strategy. To the extent that such qualities are present among professional military personnel, a twofold problem does arise: first, to minimize and counterbalance inappropriate attitudes and ways of thinking in the training and organization of the military; second, to minimize the impact of these attitudes and habits of thought on the decision-making process. These points will be reconsidered in a larger context in Chapters Four and Five.

The Military in Politics

This involvement has arisen in two ways. First, as an outgrowth of the practice of using military leaders to win and sustain support for foreign policies, generals have been drawn into debate. General Omar Bradley, who retired as Chairman of the Joint Chiefs of Staff in August 1953 and is personally devoted to the principle of military subordination in a democracy, made numerous speeches in which he tried to explain American military strategy and dispel misconceptions about it. While in most cases he was voicing military "common sense" and was merely reiterating the foreign policy of the American government, in the political environment in which he spoke his remarks were interpreted as partisan appeals, particularly as the campaign year of 1952 grew closer. The late Senator Robert Taft, a leading candidate for the Republican nomination, bitterly criticized Bradley and declared that he had "lost confidence" in the Joint Chiefs and would replace Bradley if he were elected. On April 26, 1951, he lashed out, saying that the Joint Chiefs of Staff "are absolutely under the control of the Administration," and that their recommendations "are what the Administration demands they make." He further insisted, "I have come to the point where I do not accept them as experts particularly when General Bradley makes a foreign policy speech." Bradley's condemnation of the so-called "Gibraltar theory of defense" (based primarily on air power and sea power) was felt by Taft to be a partisan attack. Actually Taft made a campaign issue of military leadership. His own cause was aided by retired and inactive generals. General Albert Wedemeyer, an air-sea-power advocate, headed a citizens-for-Taft committee, and Brigadier General Bonner Fellers, also an exponent of reliance upon air power rather than land power in the defense of Europe, served with the Republican National Committee. General MacArthur—whose foreign policy views and strategic thinking differed sharply from those of the Government—openly supported Taft and was known to be his chief military adviser.

This kind of complication did not end with the election of a new Administration. After President Eisenhower announced that the Seventh Fleet would no longer neutralize Formosa, Senator Lester Hunt (a Democrat of Wyoming) asked: "Were previous reports to Congress by Pentagon leaders their professional opinion, or were they colored by the opinions of the previous Administration? Are the new policies a reversal of previous professional estimates or are they again reflecting the policies of the new Administration?" In May 1953, the President appointed an entirely new Joint Chiefs of Staff. While Senator Taft did not recommend the new members, it is known that he strongly approved the new group—especially the Chairman, Admiral Arthur Radford, whose general strategic views the Senator shared.

Second, generals have been active in the quest for political office and have also supported candidacies other than their own. Even while he was holding the post of NATO commander, General Eisenhower, through the efforts of his supporters, became a candidate for the Republican nomination for President. From the time of his removal as United Nations commander in Korea and while still in uniform, General MacArthur made political speeches wherein he attacked the domestic and foreign policy of the Truman Adminstration and was very much in the Presidential picture. He also gave the keynote speech at the Republican National Convention in July 1952. Thus two military leaders, not yet retired, were candidates for nomination to high office and were opposed or supported by civilians and other military men in an election year when military policy and foreign policy were sharp issues.

All this happened despite United States Army Regulations (600-10) in which members are forbidden to participate in "activity at political conventions or on political committees, the making of political speeches, the publication of articles or any other public activity looking to the influencing of an election or the solicitation of votes for themselves or others."

The participation of generals in American politics is not new; the names of Washington, Jackson, Harrison, Taylor, Pierce, Grant, Hayes, and Garfield are reminders of a long tradition. As Arthur M. Schlesinger, Jr., has pointed out, what makes the present situation unique is the fact that top military officials as a group are now accepted as authorities on broad matters of public policy, are admitted to the highest national councils, and tend to be held accountable for their policy views. Generals have jumped or been dragged into the political arena, sometimes for political motives, sometimes for other reasons. The military, even when they wish to adhere to a narrow definition of their functions, no longer find it possible, apparently, to give advice unobtrusively to decision-makers. They have become decision-makers, and have ceased to be immune to political pressures. In a larger sense this change raises the issue of how far the cold war has made the nation dependent on military leadership, and of how adequate civilian leadership is.

But a more immediate issue is this: the responsible military leaders—regardless of who they are at a particular time—have a direct stake in the continuity of a minimum program for national security and in the avoidance of periodic upheavals of basic strategic concepts except where such are dictated by new conditions. Military planning must be long-range, and desired alterations will not nicely coincide with party victories. These same leaders also have a natural concern that downright false military conceptions not be permitted to circulate as part of the political coin of the realm. How can these objectives be accomplished without immersing the military in politics and without stifling free criticism? Moreover, the politicizing of generals has contributed to disunity and uneasiness among the professional military group. The emergence of "Republican" and "Democratic" generals would have significant repercussions on the functioning of this group.

The pulls in this direction are substantial. It is only natural that Congressmen who have strong convictions on military economy, the primacy of air power, the necessity of strengthening the Western Hemisphere before making sacrifices for European defense, and so on will seek support and confirmation from respected military figures, who in turn will deliberately "leak" information or talk in confidence without being willing to be quoted. Conversely, military leaders have occasion to seek support in Congress for policy views they would like to see become official. Hence military plans become election issues, and military issues are discussed in terms of political objectives which have nothing to do with foreign policy. In an extreme situation the electorate may in fact be choosing between two disagreeing camps of military planners. At the very least, military questions may not be analyzed on their merits.

Some Essential Distinctions

Before proceeding to a more detailed account of military activities which bear on foreign policy, it may be useful to discuss and clarify some frequently used phrases and to point out some of their implications.

What Is Meant by "The Military"?

The term *the military* has been used frequently in these pages. It is a shorthand term which encompasses roughly the Military Establishment organization; that is, the Defense Department and the three Service departments—Army, Navy, and Air Force—and the military and civilian personnel who serve within them. This personnel includes the civilian Secretaries who head the four Departments; the professional officers who are the uniformed heads of the Services, are in charge of the major branches and activities of the armed forces, and are, all in all, the most important and influential group within them; and finally, the great number of civilians, military officers, and enlisted men who staff the Pentagon, the training camps, the field units, and the like. It is useful to distinguish between, on the one hand, the Military Establishment organization (or one of the departments or units within it) as an agency or agencies with certain assigned tasks and responsibilities, certain resources with which to carry them out, and certain relationships to other governmental units; and, on the other hand, the civilian and military personnel who actually carry out these responsibilities and are involved in these relationships. It is also important, obviously, to distinguish at times between the professional, career military personnel of the Defense Establishment and the civilians, ranging from the Secretaries and their deputies and assistants at the top to civil servants working at lower levels in the organization. An effort will be made throughout this study to make clear in each instance in what sense the term is being used, whether in the general sense or in specific reference to one of the agencies or types of personnel noted above.

"Military Influence"

In talking about "military influence" on United States foreign policy, it is important to be clear on the distinction between the following: (a) influence of one kind or another exercised by Military Establishment personnel in various phases of foreign-policy-making, through the giving of advice or participation in the actual making of decisions; and (b) the influence on policy decisions of so-called "military" factors—values, objectives, analyses, and techniques.

The reason for this distinction is clear. Anyone—State Department officials, Congressmen, influential newspapers editors, and the general public, as well as personnel of the Defense Establishment—may be influenced by military factors in their thinking about foreign-policy problems. In other words, it is quite possible that United States foreign policy could be overbalanced toward military objectives or the use of military techniques without this necessarily being a result of Military Establishment thinking or influence. It is interesting to note that oftentimes some members of Congress are more prone to argue for quick, military solutions of problems than the high-ranking officers who testify before their committees.

"Political" and "Military" Aspects of Policy

In discussions of foreign-policy questions, a distinction is frequently made between their "political" and their "military" aspects. Since this is a widely employed dichotomy and at the same time one in which the key terms seem to be used rather loosely, with a variety of possible meanings and implications, it may be helpful to point out some of the meanings that these terms can have and why it may at times be important to be clear on the differences among them.

First, it is probably better to talk about military and nonmilitary aspects, for the following reasons. For one thing, military factors and considerations represent just one set among a whole series of factors and considerations relevant to foreign-policy-making—for example, the wide range of elements that fall under the heading of economics and finance, or of propaganda and psychological warfare. To refer to military and political aspects seems to imply that there are just these two major aspects of foreign-policy problems, and furthermore, that they are of roughly equal importance. Both of these implications would be rejected by most observers. Also, it is often assumed or implied that the so-called political aspects are the responsibility or the contribution of the civilian agencies involved, primarily the State Department in most cases. However, if the State Department is viewed as the nation's department of foreign affairs and the President's chief aid and adviser in the field of foreign policy, then the Department would seem to have a bigger job than simply advising on or being responsible for the "political" aspects of policy problems—namely, the job of synthesizing and of balancing various factors, viewpoints, and considerations, *military* and *nonmilitary*, in terms of an over-all view or "grand strategy" of American foreign policy. If this is accepted as the State Department's role in foreign policy, then the terms *military* and *nonmilitary* would seem to reflect it more accurately than *military* and *political*, with its implication that the Military Establishment and the civilian agencies are or should be fifty-fifty participants in the process.

What, then, are the possible meanings of the distinction between the *military* and *nonmilitary* aspects of foreign-policy problems?

1. It may refer to *different factors in the situation* being dealt with, and possible changes in them—perhaps to be produced by policy alternatives being considered: for example, military bases and installations, or the military capabilities of the nations involved, as contrasted with, say, their economic situations and problems, or the attitudes of their populations toward the United States. (Of course, all these factors are related to and are likely to have some impact on one another.)

2. It may refer to the *different responsibilities* of the agencies involved. That is, some aspects of the situation may seem to be closely related to or have important consequences for the responsibilities of the Military Establishment, or the State Department, or the Treasury, and so on. This distinction is obviously closely related to the first, but there may be some difference between pointing out those factors in the situation having to do with military strength and strategy and those having to do with responsibilities of the military departments.

3. A third possible meaning of the distinction is *different ways of approaching the problem* under consideration. This may mean approaching a problem with a somewhat different set of values or objectives, or perhaps a different set of priorities among them; also, different ways of interpreting or analyzing the situation— different sets of assumptions, different attitudes, different rules of interpretation or analysis. As a simplified example, a "military" approach might tend to stress the importance of obtaining certain air and naval bases overseas, with little significance attached to the political coloration of the regime being dealt with; another approach might come up with an exactly opposite appraisal.

4. Distinguishable from the third meaning but merging into it, military and nonmilitary aspects may refer to the *different skills or knowledge needed to deal with the problem*. In other words, foreign-policy problems call for a variety of information or intelligence and technical skill and knowledge, some part of which is probably possessed by some members of the Military Establishment and some part of which, one would guess, is not.

This brief four-way breakdown does not solve all the problems arising from the original distinction. There is still room for disagreement among military officers, civilian officials, and competent outside observers, among others, as to what is military and what is nonmilitary (in any of the four meanings) in any particular situation. There may be a sharp difference of opinion as to the "military" character of various factors, or anticipated consequences, in a situation, or as to their significance. There may also be some question as to the need for a military approach or for military skills and knowledge in any particular situation.

On the basis of these differences, there may also be differences as to the need for military participation in dealing with various foreign-policy problems, or if this need is accepted, as to the nature and extent of participation. The four meanings of the terms pointed out above are worth keeping in mind with regard to this latter question. It would seem to be one thing for military participation to be claimed on the basis of needed information and skills, but quite another for it to be based on fairly indirect and problematical consequences that may affect Military Establishment responsibilities. Furthermore, there is some difference between saying that the military factors and possible consequences of a situation should be carefully examined and taken into account in reaching decisions and on the other hand demanding an equal voice for, or a substantial concession to, the military approach to some situation.

Thus it seems that the precise meaning attached to these two terms in any situation may be of some consequence with regard to the nature and extent of military influence and military participation that then seems desirable or appropriate. With regard to military participation in the making of foreign policy, there is one further distinction that is both useful and important—the distinction between the *expert* and the *representational* roles played by military personnel in the process. However, since military participation is discussed and described at length in Chapter Three, discussion of this distinction is also reserved for that chapter.

chapter two

Military Organization for Foreign-Policy-Making

There is not space available in this brief study for a detailed description of the units within the Military Establishment organized to deal with foreign-policy problems.[13] The essential point to be made is that the military are so heavily and continuously involved in various phases of foreign-policy formulation and the carrying out of foreign programs that there are now units within the Defense Department and the three Service departments which are wholly concerned with these policies and programs. They work with their equivalents in civilian agencies such as the State Department and coordinate foreign-policy activities within their own departments.

The Pentagon's Foreign-Policy Units

In the Office of the Secretary of Defense there was, until the reorganization of 1953, an Assistant for International Security Affairs. Under the new Pentagon organization, he has become one of the nine Assistant Secretaries who aid the Secretary. His job is still essentially the same. He is charged with the development of recommendations and the coordination of all activities within the Military Establishment relating to international security affairs, including such matters as the NATO operations, the Pacific security treaties, and the various military-assistance programs. This job involves among other things the preparation of papers that set forth the position of the Defense Department for inter-departmentmental negotiations on policy problems, dealing with matters relating to the National Security Council, and arranging for the representation of the Defense Department on various interagency committees or international bodies. Under this official (a civilian) there are, as Professor Arthur Macmahon describes it, the following:

a military deputy, a civilian deputy who participated in the senior staff of the National Security Council, a military deputy for psychological policy, a civilian deputy for European mutual security affairs, and offices for military assistance, foreign military affairs, North Atlantic Treaty affairs, and foreign economic defense affairs. These offices were headed by men in uniform; indeed, only a small fraction of those who served there in more than routine capacities were civilians.[14]

Within each of the three Service departments, there are staff units similar to those in the Defense Department. In addition, one of the Assistant Secretaries in each department usually has general responsibility for foreign policy and international security matters. Of course specific programs are carried out by the rele-

26

vant Army, Navy, and Air Force units—procurement and supply, ordnance, transportation, and so on.

Much more could be said about these various units and activities, but what needs to be emphasized is that there are now within the military departmental organization formal staff units designed to coordinate and give guidance to its foreign-affairs activities.

One other interesting development should be noted—the National War College. Established in 1946 by the Joint Chiefs of Staff and under their direct supervision, the War College is designed to provide annually, to roughly one hundred high-ranking military officers (usually Navy captains and Army and Air Force colonels) and a small number of State Department and other civilian officials, a year's broad training in international politics and military strategy, especially as related to political policy. This is further evidence of the Military Establishment's response to its new role in the foreign-policy field. Presumably officers that have gone through the College will be better equipped to handle the increasing number of politico-military assignments both within the military organization at home and in its many activities abroad. A basic aim of the program is to increase the ability and willingness of civilian and military officials to communicate with each other, and to equip military leaders with nonmilitary knowledge and technique of analysis.[15]

The Joint Chiefs of Staff

The Joint Chiefs of Staff (JCS) are a four-man group composed of the Chief of Naval Operations, the Chiefs of Staff of the Army and the Air Force, and a Chairman (who is a high-ranking admiral or general, but does not hold a command position in his own service while Chairman). As individuals, the first three named are the uniformed heads of their Services; as a corporate body, they are the nation's top military leaders, "principal military advisers to the President, the National Security Council, and the Secretary of Defense." In recent years, the practice has developed for the Chairman of the Joint Chiefs of Staff to attend regularly all meetings of the National Security Council, although he is not a statutory member of that body.

According to the National Security Act of 1947, as amended in 1949, the responsibilities of the Joint Chiefs are as follows:

. . . Subject to the authority and direction of the President and the Secretary of Defense, the Joint Chiefs of Staff shall perform the following duties, in addition to such other duties as the President or the Secretary of Defense may direct:

(1) preparation of strategic plans and provision for the strategic direction of the military forces;

(2) preparation of joint logistic plans and assignment to military services of logistic responsibilities in accordance with such plans;

(3) establishment of unified commands in strategic areas;

(4) review of major material and personnel requirements of the military forces in accordance with strategic and logistic plans;

(5) formulation of policies for joint training of the military forces; . . .[16]

The Chiefs are supported by a number of subcommittees that deal with particular problems, but primary support is furnished by an authorized Joint Staff comprising up to 210 officers, drawn equally from the three Services and headed by a Director. This unit is responsible for the study, planning, and coordinating activities usually associated with a staff agency.

In a speech made in March 1953, when he was still Chairman of the Joint Chiefs, General Omar Bradley set forth the general foreign-policy-making role of the Joint Chiefs in these terms:

It is important to remember—and in the Joint Chiefs of Staff we are constantly reminding ourselves—that military policy and its included strategic planning is not separate and distinct from our foreign policy. The two of them are part and parcel of our over-all policy for the safety and security of our Nation.

. . . .

As the military advisers of the Government, we feel that our job is to take the various courses of action that are suggested in the problem and analyze them from the military viewpoint, telling the President, through the Secretary of Defense, what our capabilities are and as far as we know, what risks are being taken when we pursue either this course or that course.

Generally, however, I do not feel that it is Joint Chiefs of Staff responsibility to recommend specifically which course of action the Government should take. We should confine our part to pointing out the military implications and military capabilities. Then, of course, after a decision is reached, we make recommendations on the military action required to carry out such decisions. No matter what the decision becomes, once it is made we do our utmost to carry out the military responsibilities which it involves.

Perhaps some people might feel that the Joint Chiefs of Staff should stand up and resolutely and strongly recommend a national policy which we would prefer, but to date I have not been convinced that this is the proper role of the military leader. I do not believe that military strategists should choose the course of government action, and I do not believe that we should publicly, or before congressional committees, fail to support the decisions made by our civilian superiors.

In congressional hearings we feel free to give our personal opinions and to point out the same capabilities and risks that we had pointed out before any decisions were made—so that the legislators will have as full and complete information as the Secretary of Defense, and the Commander in Chief, and the Secretary of State—but I do not believe that we should go beyond this.[17]

As will be pointed out below, the Joint Chiefs of Staff have been criticized by many observers for not performing their foreign-policy role in the manner described (or prescribed) by General Bradley. However, there is no disagreement with the fact that the role of the Joint Chiefs in foreign-policy-making has been a most important one, one difficult to overestimate. There is or has been a usual procedure by which they have participated in foreign-policy decision-making: more or less important decisions—those relating to military strength or bases or military assistance, and others as well—go to the Joint Chiefs for their views and recommendations. This body also reviews the National Security Council papers which become, upon the President's approval, the official United States policy for the problem in question. The same is true of the memoranda on particular problems or decisions which are sometimes jointly prepared by the State and Defense Departments and then submitted to the President for his approval. These are, of course, in addition to the many important matters relating to the Military Establishment (such as the military budget) which go to the Joint Chiefs for their approval before moving on to the higher civilian authorities. These foreign-policy papers and memoranda are usually submitted to the Joint Chiefs even when other units in the Military Establishment have been working with the State Department and other civilian agencies on the problems in question, and may even have participated in drafting the memoranda.

In the making of foreign policy, the position of the Joint Chiefs of Staff on any issue is always something to be reckoned with, a factor not to be dismissed lightly. This is not to say that their view cannot be and has not been ignored or that they never change their minds regarding any issue. Rather, their views are not easily ignored. In fact, as has been noted by some observers, in recent years their views have tended to be accepted too quickly, too uncritically, by their civilian colleagues and superiors.

The activities of the Joint Chiefs, in the fields of both military policy and foreign policy, have been a subject of considerable comment and discussion, and even some sharp criticism. Because of the key role of the Chiefs in foreign-policy-making, the major criticisms are worth noting in some detail.

First, it is felt by some that the Chiefs have tended to act as more than advisers in their foreign-policy recommendations. Their tone has sometimes been rather peremptory, and there has often been an assumption that their recommendations would be, and should be, accepted.

A second criticism often made is that the Chiefs have tended to concern themselves too much with minor matters—matters of administrative detail within the services, and of policy implementation and detail in the field of foreign affairs. This tendency was noted in the report of the National Security Organization Task Force of the Hoover Commission in 1949, and was still a matter of concern for Vannevar Bush and retiring Defense Secretary Robert Lovett in 1952 and 1953.[18] Arthur Macmahon speaks of "congestion" at the Joint Chiefs level of the Military Establishment and cites as an example of the "incessant involvement of the Joint Chiefs in detailed determinations at each step in a program" the fact that they had to approve the exact amount of funds requested, and the exact manner in which they were allocated, for such a relatively minor matter as military assistance to Latin American countries.[19] Of course, one of the underlying assumptions of these criticisms is that to the extent that the Joint Chiefs are involved in dealing with minor details of policy and administration, they will have less time, energy, and resources available for what is presumably their fundamental task—the highest-level strategic military planning and the broad strategic direction of the armed forces of the nation.

A third major criticism made is that they have tended to be somewhat insulated from civilian control. It has been difficult for their formal civilian superiors to exercise effective control or supervision over them, for reasons of both organizational structure and an intellectual inability to take issue successfully with their judgments. More than likely there has often been an unwillingness to accept the risks and responsibilities of rejecting their supposedly expert views on matters crucial to national security.

From the organizational point of view, their corporate character has made it difficult for the Secretaries of the separate Service departments to deal with them. Their great prestige and acknowledged military wisdom have made control by the Secretary of Defense no easy task.[20] On foreign-policy matters, the State Department has not been in the most favorable position to challenge their views and recommendations.

Closely related to this point is the comment that the Joint Chiefs seem to be somewhat isolated from civilian viewpoints and ideas, both from within the Defense Establishment and outside it. This criticism was made by the Hoover Commission Task Force, and it has appeared again in recent discussions. For example, Gordon Dean, former Chairman of the Atomic Energy Commission, comments in his *Report on the Atom:*

> The Chiefs today are rather isolated from the Atomic Energy Commission, and, for that matter, from most civilian professional men such as scientists, businessmen, and those concerned with human relations. This would not be so bad if their planning were simply concerned with military maneuvers, but it isn't. Today when so much of the Joint Chiefs' planning has to do with defense mobilization, and therefore intrudes into every segment of our economy, their isolation is unfortunate.[21]

As was pointed out in Chapter One, the widespread activity of members of the Joint Chiefs and of the Joint Chiefs of Staff as a group in supporting and legitimating foreign-policy decisions and programs before Congressional committees and public audiences, in addition to participating in their development, has raised a whole series of problems and issues. It is clear that the close identification of the Joint Chiefs with particular policies and programs, as well as political parties, threatens their role as nonpartisan expert advisers. This important aspect of the Chiefs' activity will be discussed at greater length in Chapters Three and Five.

In the light of the foregoing criticisms of the Joint Chiefs of Staff, it is interesting to note the essential philosophy and concerns of the most recent reorganization of the Military Establishment, presented to Congress by President Eisenhower at the end of April 1953 and put into effect several months later. This is discussed briefly in the section that follows.

The Reorganization of 1953

There were three essential criteria or assumptions underlying the Eisenhower directive and the message to Congress that accompanied it.[22] First, stress was laid on the basic importance of civilian control, on the necessity that effective control of the Military Establishment and the major decisions regarding it rest in the hands of its politically responsible civilian leaders, acting in effect as the deputies of the President. In an effort to implement this view, increased powers in a number of areas were given to the Secretary of Defense. Furthermore, he was given additional civilian assistance in the form of six new Assistant Secretaries of Defense (there were already three Assistant Secretaries) and a general counsel of equivalent rank. The assumption was that with the help of these new civilian aides, the Secretary could better supervise and coordinate the manifold and varied activities of the three Armed Services. (This is, of course, his essential responsibility since almost all programs and operations are actually carried out by the Army, Navy, and Air Force). For the most part, these Assistant Secretaries replaced a series of joint military-civilian boards set up to deal with such problems as research and development and coordination of munitions-procurement policies; these had, apparently, not been too effective and had also tended to be dominated by their military members.

The second point stressed, and an inevitable one, was the need for the most effective and at the same time economical national-defense program possible—in other words, maximum effectiveness at minimum possible cost.

The third major concern was with the need for improved strategic planning by the Military Establishment. One important way of accomplishing this, it was felt, was to relieve the Joint Chiefs of Staff of the need to concern themselves with minor problems and administrative details. Some of the reorganization measures were designed to help in this direction, for example, the increased responsibility for managing and directing the Joint Staff given specifically to the Chairman of the Joint Chiefs (who does not have command responsibilities in one of the services). The explicitly stated purpose of these changes was that the Joint Chiefs might be "better able to perform their roles as strategic planners and military advisers."

Furthermore, since military plans must take into account "a wider range of policy and economic factors, as well as the latest developments of modern science," an effort must be made to broaden the active participation of outside persons and units in the consideration of problems before the Joint Chiefs and to bring to bear upon them more diversified skills. One procedure that is apparently going to be used for this purpose is to encourage full cooperation between the Joint Chiefs of Staff, its various subcommittees, and the Joint Staff on the one hand, and the various staff agencies in the Office of the Secretary of Defense on the other hand, in developing staff studies and papers on various problems being prepared for consideration by the Joint Chiefs. The President's message also emphasizes the importance of including within the organizational substructure of the Joint Chiefs of Staff competent civilian scientists and engineers, "outstanding civilian experts."

President Eisenhower's reorganization plan and the concerns and assumptions that underlie it seem to emphasize once again the close relation of military policy and foreign policy, of high-level military strategic thinking and planning and the larger framework of national "grand strategy." Clearly, each is dependent on the character and quality of thought of the other. That is why this stress on improved strategic planning by the Military Establishment and particularly by the Joint Chiefs, who are the nation's top military experts and advisers, is so obviously relevant to foreign-policy-making. Broad-gauged, broadly focused military strategy, plans, and advice would seem to be necessary for the most effective achievement of national security, and this modest and limited reorganization measure is just the latest in a series of organizational changes in the Military Establishment directed toward this goal since 1947.[23]

chapter three

Military Participation in Foreign-Policy-Making

In attempting to evaluate military participation in foreign-policy-making as more or less appropriate in terms of certain postulated criteria, rather detailed knowledge about this military activity seems necessary. It would be particularly convenient and useful to have reliable evidence on the number of occasions on which the military played a vital role in the formation of policy and on the precise degree of influence the miltary exerted on those occasions.

How Influential Are the Military?

Unfortunately, there is not much detailed case material available from which could be derived reasonably clear notions as to the nature of military influence on *policy substance:* that is, those situations and those problems in which the values of the military, their objectives, estimates of the situation, and analyses of policy alternatives, have tended to prove dominant, to be accepted more or less unquestioningly by their civilian colleagues; those in which the military have been able to block action on a particular decision or program; those in which the military have participated but not dominated the process; and those in which there have been sharp and explicit differences between the Pentagon and one or more civilian agencies, perhaps decided by the President in favor of the civilian agencies. About the most that is possible at this time is to offer the reader an impression of the range of activities and situations which now charac-terize military participation and may suggest the extent to which military recommendations tend to mold policy decisions. There are, however, a few instances in which reliable information of the sort suggested is available, and some of these will be noted below. First, several further points about military influence are in order.

It must be remembered that the professional officers of the defense establish-ment are, on the whole, capable and determined men, men of strong views, accustomed to positions of command. At present they have considerable prestige in the society and substantial organizational and material resources at their dis-posal. They have active public-relations units and are not without their own channels and means for influencing Congressional and public opinion. Their length of experience and security of tenure in their positions are often greater than those of the civilians with whom they deal. In other words, they have cer-tain important advantages in their relations and dealings with civilian policy-makers, members of Congress as well as State Department officials. Faced by a reluctance on the part of civilian agencies to assume certain responsibilities or an inability on their part to provide positive policy leadership, military leaders seem to be willing, if necessary, to fill the gap. Furthermore, even when faced by strong civilian leadership, there is no reason to expect them to modify their views quickly or easily.

Thus, even if the exact nature of military influence on the substance of particular policies and programs can be documented in detail only in a handful of cases, the character and extent of military participation in various phases of United States foreign-policy-making, which constitutes the main focus of interest in this chapter, is in itself important evidence of military influence. Indeed, the substantial and widespread nature of this participation is quite impressive evidence of the military's major role.

As the analysis of this chapter should make clear, military influence from situation to situation and problem to problem does not always take the same form, move through the same channels, and have similar consequences. There is, in fact, a considerable variety of situations, activities, relationships, and consequences that characterize military participation and military influence in foreign policy.

As has been suggested, there are a number of well-known cases of foreign policy activity since the end of World War II where the impact of the Military Establishment on policy substance seems clear-cut. One recent example is provided by the defense agreements signed by the United States and Spain in September 1953, under which the United States was granted the right to establish certain air and naval bases in Spain and in turn agreed to provide the Spanish Government with substantial military and economic aid. The impetus for these agreements seems to have come at least in good part from the Pentagon, and the lengthy negotiations, begun in April 1952, were conducted to a considerable extent by a military mission headed by an Air Force general. In July 1951, shortly before his death, Admiral Forrest P. Sherman, then Chief of Naval Operations, had begun exploratory discussions with the Spanish Government regarding these bases. In this instance, there would seem to be no doubt in the minds of competent observers as to the importance of the military's role.

It is also a matter of wide public knowledge that the Navy Department in 1945 and 1946 was a vigorous and strong-willed participant in the intragovernmental negotiations regarding the disposition of the Western Pacific island groups captured from the Japanese during the war and originally mandated to Japan by the League of Nations. The State Department favored placing these islands under a regular United Nations trusteeship, with the United States as the trust nation. The Navy actually preferred outright annexation, its view being that the islands were very important to American security in the Pacific, and that placing them under a United Nations trusteeship would seriously hamper their use as military and naval bases. Secretary of War Henry L. Stimson also took this view. The State Department, of course, looked at the question in terms of the United States' general position on trusteeship for colonial territories and the substantial weakening of its ability to put pressure on other colonial powers if it proceeded to annex the Japanese islands outright. The Navy, however, was not easily dissuaded, and finally, after much delay, much haggling, and many minor crises, a compromise was reached whereby the United States applied for and was granted a strategic trusteeship by the United Nations rather than a regular one, the former allowing the trust nation much greater discretion and latitude with regard to defense and fortification.[24]

In the case of the Japanese Peace Treaty, it was reported in the press by a number of newspapermen, apparently with considerable reliability, that the decision to go ahead and attempt to negotiate a peace treaty for Japan, without the Soviet Union if this proved necessary, was stalled or blocked by the Pentagon, more specifically the Joint Chiefs of Staff, from the fall of 1949 to the summer of 1950. However, the State Department was finally able to proceed with its efforts in this direction in spite of continued Pentagon doubts and reluctances, and in the end negotiated a treaty widely supported both in this country and abroad.[25]

The Sale of the Tankers, one of the public-administration case studies in the volume edited by Harold Stein, indicates clearly the role of the Navy Department and the Joint Chiefs of Staff in what started out as an effort by the State Department, in early 1947, to provide some of the Western European countries with surplus American oil tankers. In this case, however, there was an explicit, though not completely clear, statutory basis for the role of the Secretary of the Navy.[26]

These brief sketches of situations in which there is considerable data available regarding the impact of military views and preferences on policy substance should suggest the variety of patterns of military influence noted above. Obviously, if this is regarded as an area of important national concern, there is need for much more detailed documentation of this military impact. But even without it there is much to be learned from a description and analysis of the major situations and activities that characterize military participation in making and executing foreign policy, and such will be the main burden of this chapter.

The four categories to be dealt with are joint civilian-military development of policy and making of policy decisions, policy implementation, legitimation of policy, and diplomatic negotiation.

These would seem to be the four major types of formal military activity in foreign-policy-making. Perhaps mention should be made of some of the more or less informal activities, such as lobbying in Congress (for example, trying to get sympathetic Congressmen to push a military-supported policy which has not won favor at the State Department or the White House) or making public statements which seem to suggest, or frankly argue for, a line of policy different from the current official Government policy. But these would seem to be the marginal, atypical instances. Most Military Establishment activity in foreign policy falls into one of the four types to be discussed. Mention might also be made of the many important positions in the foreign-policy field held by active or retired military officers of high rank; but here again, this would seem to be peripheral to the major question of formal Military Establishment participation in the making of foreign policy.

Joint Military-Civilian Formulation of Policy

The essential development to be stressed in discussing military participation in the formulation of American foreign policy is that the Military Establishment has become a partner, a very important partner, of the State Department and other relevant civilian agencies in these policy-making activities. Furthermore, there seems to be a general understanding and acceptance of this relationship among the military and civilian personnel of the various departments involved. This would seem to be borne out by the increasing civilian-military, State-Defense cooperation, coordination, and consultation in recent years on a wide range of foreign-policy and national-security problems. Much of this cooperative activity has, inevitably, been channeled into interdepartmental committees of various sorts, both ad hoc and more or less permanent, situated at various levels in organizational hierarchies, and with varying ranges of responsibility and discretion.

Expert and Representational Functions

If one accepts the notion that the Department of State is *primus inter pares* (first among equals) in the field of foreign relations, that the Military Establishment's role is consequently secondary though important (secondary both in terms of State's primary role and the fact that its own primary problems and responsibilities are in the field of military strength and strategy) then it seems to follow that there are only two kinds of roles that military personnel can or should play in the foreign-policy-making process—the *expert* or the *representational*.

In the expert role, the military are presumably contributing to the process special skills or knowledge not otherwise available. This may consist of information, analysis and interpretation, or particular techniques. As experts, their position is presumably advisory, and they bear no formal responsibility for the decisions taken on the basis of their advice. Equally, there is no basis on which they can *demand* that they be invited to participate or *demand* that their views be heeded. They are in the position of being consulted as to their views and recommendations. The advice which they offer can be judged on its merits, *not* on the basis of the power of those who offer it.

In the *representational* role, on the other hand, their essential contribution to the process is not expert knowledge, but rather representation of departmental interests and responsibilities. The problem being dealt with is presumably so intimately related to the interests and assigned responsibilities of the Defense Department or one of the armed services that they either claim or in any case are granted representation in the group dealing with the problem and thus share responsibility for the decisions reached. If the problem is a continuing one, there would seem to be almost a right to participate, and during participation a right to join in the decisions reached, and presumably to block the choice of disapproved alternatives. When acting as Military Establishment representatives in joint civilian-military policy-making, the military personnel are in effect members of a cooperative enterprise in which they have a recognized authority, rather than expert advisers to be consulted if the civilian agencies so desire.

There are a number of comments to be made on this expert-representational distinction. First, these are obviously ideal types. The roles tend in practice to shade off into one another. For example, what starts out as participation on an expert adviser basis becomes so formalized that the expectation of consulting and of being consulted develops into something accepted and normal. What results after a while is a situation in which the military personnel are in effect representing their agencies, and there is no thought of excluding them even if the problem at hand does not seem to call for special military knowledge or expertise. As a matter of fact, it might be said that while the original rationale for military participation in the making of foreign policy rested essentially on the need for their special skills and knowledge in certain areas, in most present-day instances of joint military-civilian activity in foreign-policy-making the typical military role tends to be closer to the representational than to the expert. This is not to say that military expertise is no longer being contributed to the process, but rather that it is probably more and more being contributed in situations where the military have the rights and responsibilities of representation rather than the more circumscribed role of offering expert advice and information when called upon.[27]

If the military have tended to move steadily from an expert role to a representational role, it does not necessarily follow that the shift in kind of influence has been formally recognized and sanctioned by statutes, executive orders, and administrative rulings. On the contrary, it is entirely probable that in many cases routinization of civil-military relations has not been so recognized. However, habit and precedent can be just as binding as formal rules. This transition from expertise to representation has been furthered by the fact that in many situations in which the military and civilians are thrown together, the civilians have no real choice but to accept the military's information and interpretation. In this case, the military are no longer expert advisers but have become in effect policy-making equals. Thus civilian supremacy may be weakened either in formally recognized relationships or in relationships which have resulted from routine. The weakening is not necessarily the result of anyone's plot. There seem to be two basic reasons why talented, strong-minded civilian officials may feel helpless in the face of military expertise, thus in effect endowing the military with representational prerogatives: first, the civilians rarely have reliable alternative sources of information about military matters despite the fact that military groups do not always agree; second, the civilians lack the experience and knowledge of military thinking which would enable them to challenge successfully the interpretations of military experts. Intelligent officials seldom like to argue from positions of weakness, that is, from positions not based on knowledge which is reliable or accepted as reliable. If a competent civilian career official can do nothing more on occasion than "accept" the military view, the Congressman who is a member of an appropriations committee is perhaps even less well off. Budget control is in theory an effective device for guaranteeing civilian supremacy, but budget procedures may leave the Representative or Senator helpless before the mass of technical information presented by the military leaders.

The Military as Expert Advisers

The most important example of the military-as-experts role in making foreign policy is provided by the Joint Chiefs of Staff. Since their function as top military advisers to the President, the Secretary of Defense, and the National Security Council has already been discussed in Chapter Two, it need only be added that even in the case of the Joint Chiefs, as some commentators have noted, elements of the representational have tended to slip into their role. That is, there has apparently developed on their part some expectation of being consulted regularly on a wide range of matters of greatly varying importance and, on the part of civilian leaders, an accompanying unwillingness to proceed without consulting the Joint Chiefs. One possible consequence of such participation by the Joint Chiefs in matters where they have no special expertness to contribute might be to reduce the general quality and usefulness of their contributions when they were highly relevant. Furthermore, as has been suggested, to the extent that they are viewed as having a responsible voice in the decisions reached, they are likely more and more to be held politically accountable for their views, particularly in a period when issues of foreign policy and national security are dominant ones for the nation. However, by statutory prescription, general agreement, and the statements of the Joint Chiefs themselves, their role in national security and foreign-policy-making is essentially that of expert advisers.

This is probably the appropriate point to mention another contribution of the Military Establishment to making foreign policy which fits more or less into the expertise category; that is, the provision of intelligence and information. This may be in the form of "raw data," or perhaps the analysis and interpretation of problems and situations. The Military Establishment, of course, has its own units for gathering intelligence and evaluating it. Each service in fact has its own intelligence branch. The military attachés assigned to American embassies and legations abroad comprise one part of these intelligence organizations.

Thus the Defense Establishment, through its representatives on various interdepartmental committees, but primarily through the circulation of copies of reports, dispatches, and other intelligence data to the State Department and other interested government agencies, feeds into the foreign-policy decision-making process information and analyses on a wide range of matters, from those specifically dealing with the military capabilities of other nations to broader questions of their policy intentions and basic strengths and weaknesses.

Military Representation in Policy Development

As has already been said, military-civilian cooperation and coordination in foreign-policy decision-making goes on at various organizational levels and in a variety of ways, informal as well as formal, over the telephone or at lunch as well as in working groups and committees. But granted the existence and the importance of the informal and the casual, the formal and the regular would seem to provide the basic structure of cooperation.

At the very top of this structure is the National Security Council (NSC) established in 1947 by the National Security Act. At the present time this Cabinet-level committee is the highest-level unit in the United States Government concerned with the major dimensions of American foreign policy and national security. From this point of view, and because it has become increasingly active and effective in the last few years, it is undoubtedly the most important single unit dealing with American "grand strategy" and the foreign policies and programs that implement it. Indeed, by statutory prescription the Council is supposed "to advise the President with respect to the integration of domestic, foreign, and military policies relating to the national security so as to enable the military services and the other departments and agencies of the Government to cooperate more effectively in matters involving the national security," and as previously noted, "to assess and appraise the objectives, commitments, and risks of the United States in relation to our actual and potential military power."[28]

It would be safe to say that at present the National Security Council advises the President with regard to all the major decisions he must make in the wide realm of national security and foreign policy. For example, the proposed Military Establishment budget for the fiscal year 1954–55 was an important matter for Council discussion in the fall of 1953. Presumably the major decision to go ahead with the development and construction of a hydrogen bomb was considered by the Council. All of the major foreign policies and programs of the United States in the last four or five years have probably been on the Council's agenda at one time or another, and many of the major decisions regarding these are probably embodied in National Security Council policy papers which, when approved by the President, represent official United States policy.

Under the present law, the Council has five statutory members. Others can be added if the President desires, to serve at his pleasure. In addition to the President, there are the following: the Vice-President, the Secretary of State, the Secretary of Defense, and the Director of Defense Mobilization. Under President Truman, the Secretary of the Treasury and the Director of the Mutual Security Agency (now the Foreign Operations Administration) were also regular members, and this arrangement has apparently been continued by President Eisenhower. Also in attendance, in an advisory capacity, are the Chairman of the Joint Chiefs of Staff and the Director of the Central Intelligence Agency. The Central Intelligence Agency, the nation's top intelligence organization, is under the general direction of the Council and reports directly to it; the same was true of the Psychological Strategy Board until it was disbanded in September 1953.

The National Security Council is situated organizationally in the Executive Office of the President and has its own small executive secretariat whose head works closely with the President. Under President Eisenhower, the Council has even increased somewhat in importance. It meets more frequently, and its supporting groups have been strengthened to some extent. For example, until the changes instituted by Mr. Eisenhower, there was a committee composed of sub-Cabinet-level officials from each of the agencies represented on the Council which did a great deal of preparatory and planning work for it. This group was called the Senior Staff; its State Department representative, for example, was the director of the very important Policy Planning Staff. Also attached to this unit were advisers from the Office of the Joint Chiefs of Staff, from the Central Intelligence Agency, and from the Psychological Strategy Board. The members of the Senior Staff were officials with full-time positions in their own agencies, which thus limited the amount of time they could give to the work of the Council. The Senior Staff has now been replaced by a similarly constituted group called the Planning Board. There are, however, these differences. First, members of the Board were directed to make the Security Council their primary task. Second, the President's own special assistant for national-security affairs was made chairman of the group. Finally, the Board is to meet more frequently than the Senior Staff did.

As a final step, President Eisenhower has replaced the old Psychological Strategy Board with a new group called the Operations Coordinating Board. This is a five-man committee including representatives of the State and Defense Departments, the Foreign Operations Administration, the Central Intelligence Agency, and a special Presidential assistant concerned with psychological strategy. Apparently the purpose of this group, which is under the chairmanship of the Undersecretary of State, is to coordinate all the foreign policies, programs, and activities of the United States so that maximum advantage is gained from them psychologically and propagandawise as well as in other ways.

President Eisenhower's apparent interest in the National Security Council and his intention to rely quite heavily upon it point up an interesting bit of historical background. It is the fact that the original impetus for the establishment of the National Security Council came from the armed forces. In fact until 1949 the three Service Secretaries as well as the Defense Secretary were statutory members of the Council. It was felt, however, that this situation tended to result in an overbalance toward the military point of view so the three Service Secretaries were dropped when the National Security Act was amended in 1949. There has been no serious suggestion in recent years that the deliberations and activities of the National Security Council and its subordinate units are dominated by the Pentagon. However, a description of the organization and the functions of this most important agency makes clear that the Military Establishment (through the Secretary of Defense, the Joint Chiefs of Staff, and their deputies and assistants) is well represented on it.[29]

Below the Council level, there are a considerable number of interdepartmental committees on which the military are represented. One example of a fairly high-level unit was the committee composed of representatives from the Defense Department, State Department, and Economic Cooperation Administration which coordinated the activities of these agencies in the Mutual Security Aid program (involving both military and economic aid) until this task was assigned in 1951 to the Director of the Mutual Security Agency (which replaced the Economic Cooperation Administration). While none of the military departments are statutory members of the National Advisory Council on International Monetary and Financial Problems (NAC), a Cabinet-level committee, Defense Department representatives have worked on some of its staff subcommittees, for example, the group dealing with the problem of repayment of Government and Relief in Occupied Areas (GARIOA) grants by Germany and Japan. The participation of the military is probably explained by the fact that the GARIOA grants program was actually administered by the Army.

As further evidence of the importance of the interdepartmental committee, Professor Macmahon notes that in 1951 the Department of State was represented on 130 interdepartmental units of various kinds. Twenty-one of these dealt with politico-military policy (and it can therefore be assumed that the Military Establishment was also represented), sixteen dealt with security and intelligence, and sixteen with economic and military assistance.[30]

In some cases, where they are the only agencies importantly involved, the State and Defense Departments have set up joint committees or working groups to deal with particular problems or issues. For example, in the case of the peace treaty for Japan and the three related Pacific security pacts, a great deal of the technical work, such as drafting or revising treaty articles, was done by working groups of middle-level officials, often State Department desk officers and Army colonels, of the Defense, Army, and State Departments. Naturally, those issues on which these groups cannot agree are referred to higher levels, which may mean the Assistant Secretary or the Undersecretary. Another aspect of State-Military cooperation in foreign-policy-making is illustrated by the fact that in the course of negotiations and activities leading to the Japanese Peace Treaty, John Foster Dulles, then Special Ambassador charged with responsibility for this problem, had a number of conversations at the Pentagon regarding it with various high civilian and military officials, including the Joint Chiefs of Staff.

As already briefly noted, the procedure often followed when only the State Department and the Military Establishment are dealing with some problem, and it does not call for the attention of the National Security Council, is for the two agencies to draft a joint memorandum for the President which is signed by the State and Defense Secretaries and submitted to the Chief Executive for his approval. In the infrequent cases of disagreement, the nature of the differences and the supporting arguments for each position are summarized for the President, who must then make the decision.

It is obviously impossible to capture the full flavor of military-civilian cooperation and coordination in the formulation of American foreign policy without actually reading some of the jointly drafted documents and memoranda and sitting in on some of the joint committees and working groups. However, there are a number of basic points that should be kept in mind. First of all, there has been no intention to imply that all always goes smoothly, that there is always complete understanding and complete agreement among the military and civilian agencies involved. Sometimes, perhaps inevitably, agreement is reached at the price of vagueness, of postponing the essential decision, or of what would seem to be undesirable compromise on the policy issues in question. Sometimes there is in effect a breakdown in communication and in coordinating activities. Nevertheless the fundamental development to be kept in mind is that Military Establishment participation in the formulation of foreign policy and in the making of important foreign-policy decisions has become pretty generally accepted by all concerned, and that there are now formalized and routinized channels and agencies for necessary military-civilian consultation, coordination, and cooperation, familiar to the officials involved and generally employed by them.

Policy Implementation

It is not possible to draw a strict line between the development and formulation of policies on the one hand and their execution and implementation on the other. In the process of carrying out policy directives a certain amount of interpretation and discretionary action is inevitable. Such action will not always represent what the policy-makers themselves had in mind. Directives are sometimes drafted in rather vague and general terms, because of departmental differences regarding the policy, or perhaps through inadequate thought or analysis on the part of the policy-makers. To the extent that this is the case, those who are carrying out the policy have greater burdens of decision and interpretation, but at the same time a wider discretion to make policy on their own.

Sometimes in the process of policy execution—perhaps most of the time—problems or difficulties arise which had not been anticipated by the policy-makers. The manner in which these situations are dealt with by those carrying out the policies may result in important changes in the purposes and procedures of the policies as originally conceived. It may even result in substantial modification of the original policy directive.

It is clear, then, that there is a close relation between policy formulation and policy implementation, that the one reacts upon the other, that the official who implements policy is usually doing something more than mechanically carrying out his orders, sometimes substantially more. All of this granted, there is still a useful distinction to be made between the centers of foreign-policy decision-making and the various places and situations in which policies and programs are being put into effect. And the Military Establishment is and has been at least as heavily involved in carrying out important foreign-policy programs of the United States as in participating in the making of high-level foreign-policy decisions.

It goes without saying that the conduct of active warfare by the armed forces is a most vital and significant carrying out of American foreign policy. But when this has occurred in the past on a major scale, the military effort has become the major focus of attention and the major foreign-relations activity of the nation. In the case of the Korean War, we have seen a major military operation carried on as a "limited war" and regarded as just one important problem or situation in the foreign-policy field to be dealt with along with a number of others. In fact, a major concern of most American policy-makers has been to prevent the war from assuming too large a role, from limiting the freedom and flexibility of American policy and demanding too large a commitment of American resources. A major war on the continent of Asia against large Asian armies has been regarded as "the wrong war at the wrong place, at the wrong time, and with the wrong enemy."[81] Nevertheless, as was pointed out in Chapter One, the military operations and the decisions by the military field commanders in Korea have had implications and consequences ranging far beyond the tactical situation there. The great variety and intensity of emotions aroused by the actions of General MacArthur, both in the United States and in the nations of the West allied with it, are in themselves strong tribute to this fact. It must also be remembered that the Korean War was fought under the banner of the United Nations, that the American Commander in Chief commanded an international army and made periodic reports to the Security Council of the United Nations. The Korean War provides the most obvious, and probably the most important, recent example of foreign-policy implementation by the military.

Occupation of Ex-Enemy Nations

One of the most important tasks of the Military Establishment for a number of years after the end of World War II was the occupation and control of the defeated enemy countries, principally Germany and Japan. Some observers have argued that these were not appropriate responsibilities for the military, that general direction of these countries should have been placed in the hands of the State Department or some other civilian agency shortly after the end of the war. Leaving this question aside for the time being, it seems clear that certain consequences followed from these military responsibilities. For one thing, the military had a substantial role in the development of policy for Germany and Japan. Another interdepartmental committee, the State-War-Navy Coordinating Committee (SWNCC), was originally responsible for policy-making in this area, but after a time the task fell to the two agencies principally concerned, the State and Army Departments. The Army had a staff unit, the Civil Affairs Division, to deal with occupation and related matters. In addition, one of the Army Assistant Secretaries usually had general supervision over military government and occupied-areas affairs and responsibility for the development of Defense Establishment policy positions on these matters. As might be expected, the Army Department at home developed considerable knowledge and expertness about the occupied areas, and considerable interest and concern in them, as a result of these responsibilities.[82] Being in full charge of carrying out the high-level policy directives regarding Germany and Japan, the Army of course had a certain discretionary power which was increased by the extent to which the State Department and itself could not reach agreement on high-level policy. The State Department, naturally, had no direct chain-of-command control over the Army's generals in charge of the occupations.

Furthermore, thanks to the power of a field commander under the Army organizational structure, there developed in the occupied areas, especially in Japan, what amounted to second and separate military agencies with knowledge, expertise, and decided views about these countries and what would be desirable American policies regarding them. In 1950, General MacArthur had a headquarters staff, concerned solely with occupation as distinct from military matters, of more than 2,000 people, largely civilian employees, but with most of the top positions in the dozen or so staff sections held by military officers. In MacArthur's case these factors, combined with his own strong personality and ambitions and his considerable public and political support in the United States, made him a most important figure in the development of American policy toward Japan, and for the Far East generally.[33] While General Lucius D. Clay, American Military Commander in Germany, did not have the advantage of complete and undivided American control such as General MacArthur in effect had in Japan, it is generally agreed that he also played an important role in the development of American postwar policy toward Germany.

There is no doubt that the Pentagon would have been involved in any case in the development and execution of United States policy in the occupied countries, because the policing and similar duties in these countries called for the stationing therein of substantial American armed forces. Also, both Germany and Japan were industrially and strategically of great importance, and this would necessarily have concerned the military. It can still be said with assurance, however, that the Army's responsibility for the direct control and occupation of the defeated enemy countries for an extended period of time increased considerably the impact of the Military Establishment on American postwar policies toward these countries.[34]

Peacetime Military Missions Abroad

To return to those responsibilities more closely related to military strength and strategy, there are at present American military missions in a large number of countries all over the world, engaged first in estimating their military needs and making recommendations for shipments of American military equipment to them, and then in helping their armed forces to learn to use this equipment when it arrives and, more generally, aiding in the training and building up of the armed forces of nations friendly with or allied to the United States.

These military missions of course operate within a larger framework of allocations provided by Congressional appropriations and policy decisions made by high-level officials in the executive branch. According to the Mutual Security Act of 1952, the Secretary of Defense has primary responsibility and authority for:

(1) the determination of military end-item requirements; (2) the procurement of military equipment in a manner which permits its integration with service programs; (3) the supervision of end-item use by the recipient countries; (4) the supervision of the training of foreign military personnel; and (5) the movement and delivery of military end-items.

Furthermore, while the apportionment of funds between countries is to be determined by the President, the Secretary of Defense is responsible for "the establishment of priorities in the procurement, delivery and allocation of military equipment."[35]

The most important part of the military-assistance program consists of military aid to the NATO countries of Europe. In each of these countries there is a Military Assistance Advisory Group, consisting of representatives of the three Armed Services, which carries out the tasks noted above. The program they recommend for each country must of course be fitted into the over-all military-assistance program, as decided upon by the Defense Secretary, the Joint Chiefs of Staff, the NATO Commander in Chief and other high military and civilian officials of the Defense Establishment in conjunction with the State Department, the Foreign Operations Administration, the Bureau of the Budget, and of course the President.

Another important aspect of the build-up of military (and economic) strength in Western Europe which is under the direct control of the Military Establishment is the so-called "offshore procurement" program whereby the United States has been purchasing military equipment in Western Europe (and elsewhere to a lesser extent) for provision to other countries or even to the producing countries themselves.

Military training missions have played significant roles in some European countries. For example, the American military mission to Greece under General James A. Van Fleet was given considerable credit for the strengthening of the Greek Army which enabled that force to defeat finally the strong guerrilla army of the local Greek Communist movement after several years of rather unsuccessful mountain fighting. Similarly, the American military mission in Turkey, and the substantial military and economic aid sent to that country, have been viewed as important contributors to Turkey's increasing military strength and economic stability. Large quantities of military equipment have also gone from the United States to Yugoslavia, and high-ranking American and Western European officers, as well as members of the military mission, have on occasion inspected Yugoslav forces, observed their maneuvers, and attempted to evaluate their employment of the military equipment sent to them.

American military assistance and training groups have also been active in the Middle East and the Far East. For several years there has been an important military mission on the island of Formosa, seat of the Chinese Nationalist Government, and its present chief, Major General William Chase, because of his occasional public statements and speeches, is probably better known than the American Ambassador there, Karl Rankin. The importance of this group, responsible for training the forces of Chiang Kai-shek, and also estimating their effectiveness and probable battleworthiness, is clear. Perhaps even more important and closely related to larger political and diplomatic problems is the work that has been done and is being done by elements of the Eighth Army in Korea in the training of Republic of Korea divisions. The increasing strength of these units may allow the reduction of American land forces in Korea; on the other hand, this strength may embolden the South Koreans to drive into North Korea on their own, with possible consequences as far-reaching as that of starting World War III. Apparently the American program of military assistance to these and other Far Eastern countries had become important enough to call for a three-week inspection trip to the Orient in early 1953 by Major General George H. Olmsted, at that time Director of the Defense Department's Office of Military Assistance. Upon his return to Washington, the General had comments to make on a number of matters relating to American policy in the Far East besides the military-assistance programs.[36]

Military assistance to other nations and the training of their armed forces have resulted in considerable activity by members of the Military Establishment, from the Defense Secretary and the Joint Chiefs of Staff to the personnel of the various missions abroad—activity with important political and economic as well as military consequences, involving military officials in close and continuing relationships with high military and political leaders of other nations. In Western Europe the agency organizing and unifying much of this activity has been the North Atlantic Treaty Organization (NATO) and particularly its Army, directed from a central, internationally staffed headquarters near Paris. Here too, as already suggested in Chapter One, the personnel of the Military Establishment, both civilian and military, have played a most important role.

The North Atlantic Treaty Organization

The NATO Army probably represents the first important instance of the peacetime organization of an international army with a regular commander in chief, appropriately staffed and operating at his own headquarters, who reports to and is responsible to a Council of the participating nations (composed in this case of their foreign ministers). The three American generals who have held the post of Supreme Allied Commander, Europe (SACEUR) have been almost as much political and diplomatic as military leaders. This is strikingly illustrated by the first annual Supreme Commander's Report issued by General Eisenhower in April 1952. The lengthy document covered the whole range of contemporary Europe's basic problems, from the need for higher standards of living and for economic and political unity to the importance of incorporating West Germany into the European defense system.[37] General Eisenhower probably spent as much time with European political and economic leaders as with European admirals and generals. At times General Eisenhower and his successors have warned European leaders of the dangers of delay, of the failure to build up armed strength quickly. Their comments have ranged far beyond what might be thought of as the military sphere. Even General Ridgway, who was supposedly inclined to minimize the extramilitary aspects of his role, was reported to have made a "fervent and specific appeal" for the ratification of the European Defense Community agreements during a visit with West German Chancellor Konrad Adenauer in Bonn in September 1952.[38]

Considerable American air, sea, and land forces are included in the various NATO commands and armies. Some of the large NATO commands are headed by American admirals and generals. Of course a large number of Americans work with personnel of other nations at the SHAPE staff headquarters near Fontainebleau. The American Defense Establishment is also represented at higher levels in the NATO organization. When the NATO Council was first organized, the defense and finance ministers of the nations involved met apart from the foreign ministers in the so-called Defense and Finance Committees. At the most recent meetings of the Council, all three groups met jointly, with the foreign minister heading each national delegation. Accompanying Secretary of State Dulles to the Paris meeting in December 1953 were Secretary of Defense Charles Wilson and Secretary of the Treasury George Humphrey, as well as Foreign Operations Administration chief Harold Stassen. These four officials were also accompanied by a staff of civilian and military aides.

Reporting to the NATO Council is a Military Committee made up of top-ranking officers of each country. The present American representative is the former Chief of Staff of the Army, General J. Lawton Collins. General Collins is also the American representative on the Standing Group, made up of British, French, and American officers, that meets in Washington and acts in effect as the executive committee of the Military Committee. The Standing Group and the Military Committee work closely, of course, with SACEUR and his staff.

Overseas Bases

Headquarters, committees, and standing groups do not carry much military weight unless they have at their command appropriate trained forces and matériel. For this reason there are substantial numbers of American troops now stationed at overseas bases in many parts of the world. Many of them are stationed in the territories of other sovereign nations—Britain, France, Japan, the Philippines—or in their colonial possessions, for example, French North Africa; and their presence in these areas raises a whole series of questions and problems, usually minor but capable of proving troublesome, for both the "sending" and the "receiving" countries. For the sake of the maximum security and efficiency of these bases, and also for the sake of generally amicable relations between the United States and the other countries concerned, it would seem to be important that the local populations be kept more or less friendly, or at the least not too strongly hostile, in their attitudes toward these American forces. This would seem to be a continuing responsibility and problem both for the American military officers in command and for the American diplomatic representatives in the "receiving" countries.[39]

There are other more specific and at times difficult problems. For example, there is the matter of criminal jurisdiction, which was the subject of considerable attention in Status of Forces agreements with the NATO countries and Japan, and also on the floor of the United States Senate. It is essentially the question of which nation shall have jurisdiction over soldiers committing crimes off the base and while not on duty. It is understandable that the host countries would want the right to try these soldiers in their own courts; on the other hand, military officers prefer to have their personnel under their control to the greatest extent possible. This is clearly not a major issue; the number of men involved is not likely to be large. It has, however, proved to be something of a problem. For example, the Japanese were particularly sensitive on this score because of the long Oriental fight against extraterritoriality for Westerners and because of the recently ended American occupation. On the other hand, some United States Senators have been a bit wary about leaving American soldiers "at the mercy" of foreign courts with foreign laws and customs. Under the agreements concluded in recent years with Japan and the NATO countries, criminal jurisdiction was essentially granted to the "receiving" countries.[40]

Criminal jurisdiction is one of the more difficult problems. Another is provided by the varying consequences that the presence of American forces may have on the local economy. They may be a boon; on the other hand, they can contribute by their spending to inflationary pressures. All in all, it is probably expecting too much to hope that the American forces stationed abroad will actually increase American popularity in these nations. However, there is no doubt that their activities can have considerable effect on larger American relations with these nations, and thus the officers commanding these forces would seem to have some diplomatic and political as well as strictly military tasks on their hands if they are to make the best of what traditionally has always been less than the happiest of relationships.

The Problem of Coordination

Running through most of these military activities which carry out American policies and programs abroad are several basic problems. One of these is the need for appropriate coordination and cooperation with the various civilian agencies carrying out American policies in foreign countries—with the chief American diplomatic representative and his staff, the economic-aid missions, officials with regional responsibilities and assignments, and American representatives on various regional and international organizations. There are problems of continuing and reliable channels of communication, of reasonably clear allocation of powers and responsibilities among the various units and agencies, of assuring the compatibility of the various programs and their continued progress in the same general direction. To make clear the difficulty of this problem of coordination and cooperation it would be enough merely to list the missions to foreign countries, the regional representatives and organizations, and the representatives on the many international bodies in Western Europe in recent years of the State Department, the Mutual Security Agency (or the Foreign Operations Administration), the Military Establishment, and other agencies.

Without a doubt, this problem puts considerable additional burdens on Military Establishment personnel. They not only must carry out their military assignments successfully, but also must be aware of the relation of these to other foreign-policy operations and of the wider implications of their activities and decisions. In sum, the military are at present involved in a considerable number of overseas activities and operations of great importance to American foreign policies and relations, with consequences and implications going far beyond the bounds of military strength and strategy narrowly viewed. Clearly this means heavy and perhaps unfamiliar burdens for the military personnel carrying them out.

Legitimation of Policy

As was remarked earlier, one of the noteworthy aspects of the processes that characterize recent American foreign-policy decision-making is the use of members of the Defense Establishment, both top civilian officials and the Joint Chiefs of Staff and other high-ranking military officers, to testify in support of new foreign policies and programs and the continuance of ongoing ones before committees of Congress. With regard to the professional officers, this testimony has seemed in some cases to deal with questions and problems outside the realm of expert military knowledge or competence or obvious tasks and responsibilities of the Military Establishment. As a matter of fact, the practice of using such officers to help legitimate policies, i.e., to help get them accepted in Congress and throughout the country, raises important questions, which will be discussed in Chapters Four and Five.

Numerous illustrations of the practice can be cited. The following, it might be noted, are taken more or less at random and could be multiplied substantially with little effort. General Omar Bradley was one of the military officers most active in appearing before Congressional committees and in making public addresses on United States policy. This is particularly interesting in view of the fact already noted, that he has been one of the military men most self-conscious about the limited role of the military in national-policy-making and most insistent on the importance of civilian supremacy in the American Government. On May 7, 1953, General Bradley appeared before the House Foreign Affairs Committee to testify in support of the Administration's Mutual Security Program, comprising economic as well as military aid to foreign nations, for the fiscal year of 1953–54. Explaining that his was a "strictly military viewpoint" on this program, he indicated that there was no evidence that the Soviet threat to the "free world" had diminished in any way; and that the NATO nations were making as great an effort as they could under present conditions. He therefore stressed the importance to American and "free world" security of continuing the Mutual Security Program in both its economic and military aid aspects.[41] The General appeared before the Senate Foreign Relations Committee on January 21, 1952, to testify on behalf of the peace treaty for Japan and the three related Pacific security arrangements. In a letter written earlier to Senator Arthur Watkins (Republican, Utah), Bradley had stated that the Defense Department and the Joint Chiefs of Staff had been "freely and constantly consulted" during the preparation of the peace treaty, that "essentially" the peace treaty was drawn in terms which did not contain within themselves "the seeds of another war," and that the Joint Chiefs were "of the opinion that this treaty, along with the proposed United States-Japanese security treaty, which should come into force simultaneously, will provide the United States the maximum security obtainable in the Far East at this time." In the course of the Senate hearings, John Foster Dulles, when asked for the State Department's views on whether the terms of the peace treaty, especially with regard to southern Sakhalin and the Kurile Islands, met United States security requirements in the Pacific, referred the questioner to General Bradley's letter to Senator Watkins. (The letter was also made a part of the record of the hearings.) At the close of his testimony, General Bradley affirmed under Senatorial questioning that the several treaties did contribute "very materially" to the maintenance of peace in the Pacific and that the treaties would contribute beneficially to Japan as well as to the United States.[42] This particular testimony raises an interesting point, again reserved for discussion in Chapter Five.

General Bradley also testified in support of the North Atlantic Treaty when it was being considered by the Senate Foreign Relations Committee in May 1949. He pointed out the military advantages that the United States would gain from the pact and the related military-assistance program. At the same time he set forth briefly the larger policy of which the treaty formed a part and said that he had no doubt that given the assurance of aid and the means to resist, the European countries would resolutely contest any threat of aggression.[43]

In the joint hearings of the Armed Services and Foreign Relations Committees of the Senate on the "Military Situation in the Far East," called forth by President Truman's relief of General MacArthur in April 1951, Bradley testified along with the other members of the Joint Chiefs, Generals Collins and Vandenberg and Admiral Sherman, and Secretary of Defense General George C. Marshall. These military leaders, it was generally agreed, played the major role in defending the Truman Administration against strong attacks upon it for its Far Eastern policy and for its dismissal of MacArthur from his Far Eastern Command. They supported the President's action in relieving the General, presented evidence that the General had taken actions going beyond his orders and his assigned responsibilities and contrary to official policy, and generally argued in favor of the current United States policy in Korea and the Far East.[44]

General MacArthur's address to a joint session of Congress on his return was of course not sponsored by the Administration and not designed to support Administration policies. However, a little more than a year later MacArthur's successor, General Matthew Ridgway, after returning from his assignment in Tokyo, spoke before a joint session of the House and Senate on Korea and Japan. In addition to a survey of the military operations of the Eighth Army while under his personal and, later, general command, he commented on the armistice negotiations then going on and devoted a good part of his address to a broad-ranging analysis of the situation of Japan and of United States relations with that country. All in all, his speech is a document worth looking at for anyone interested in American policy in the Far East.[45]

It goes without saying that the Secretary of Defense, the three civilian Service Secretaries, and their deputies appear to testify before Congressional committees on behalf of foreign-policy programs. Such activities on their part would seem to raise fewer problems than in the case of the professional officers, since these officials are, after all, politically appointed and politically responsible. One recent appearance, however, by one of them, Assistant Secretary of Defense Frank Nash (in charge of international security affairs) was particularly interesting as an indication of the wide range of interests and responsibilities of the Defense Establishment. Mr. Nash testified on April 8, 1953, before a subcommittee of the Senate Judiciary Committee considering Senator Bricker's proposed amendment to the Constitution to limit further the powers of the executive branch to negotiate international treaties and agreements. He made clear his opposition to the Bricker amendment, noting that it would hamstring the Military Establishment in its activities abroad, and pointed to the truce negotiations then going on in Korea as one clear example.[46]

In addition to their many other tasks, it has apparently now become customary to call on the NATO Supreme Commanders for testimony to support the continuance and proposed size of the yearly Mutual Security Programs. For example, when in the spring of 1952 the Senate Foreign Relations Committee was seriously discussing a cut in foreign-aid appropriations for 1952–53, General Eisenhower on May 3, 1952, sent a letter to the chairman of the Committee to the effect that a substantial reduction in foreign aid might threaten the success of the whole program. More recently, the NATO Commanders have flown over from Paris to Washington to testify before the relevant House and Senate committees in support of the Mutual Aid Programs. Newspaper comments prior to General Ridgway's arrival for this purpose in Washington in late May 1953 indicated that his testimony was regarded quite consciously by people both in Congress and in the executive branch as an attempt to bolster the Administration's case for the aid program.[47]

One might say that this role for the Supreme Commander was initiated by General Eisenhower, who upon his return from a European inspection trip just after his appointment as SACEUR, spoke to an informal session of both houses of Congress in the Library of Congress auditorium and set forth what was in effect a broadly focused exposition of the contemporary situation in Europe and a quite impressive explanation and defense of American policies in that area.[48]

The military's activities in support of American foreign policy have not been limited to appearances before Congress. They have also been quite active in presenting their views to wider public audiences. Of course their testimony before Congress may get some public attention to the extent that it is widely reported in the press. However, this is by no means the only outlet for their views. They are featured speakers at important conventions, meetings, and dinners. They appear on national radio and television programs. They make statements to the press and hold widely reported press conferences. They are granted honorary degrees by colleges and universities and make appropriate commencement or other addresses. It is rare for a day to go by without the report of some speech or statement by a military officer in the press.

Examples are accordingly not difficult to find. Within a recent one-month period there were at least the following speeches by military officers reported in the newspapers. On October 24, 1953, General Ridgway spoke at Lafayette College, stressing the need for the further build-up of the NATO forces, especially their manpower, in spite of the new weapons being developed. Less than three weeks later, the General (now Army Chief of Staff) spoke at Hofstra College, where he received an honorary degree, and warned that the Soviet forces threatening American security "knew no scruples or restraint except the fear of effective retaliation and defeat." Earlier, on October 8, General Alfred M. Gruenther, the present NATO Commander, speaking at the Alfred E. Smith Memorial Foundation dinner in New York, had warned against succumbing to the Soviet peace offensive or faltering in the defense of Western Europe. It was also reported that he was to appear on a major radio and television interview program on Sunday of the same week before flying back to Paris. Army officers did not represent the only active voice of the Pentagon; on October 22, Admiral Robert B. Carney, Chief of Naval Operations, addressed the National Press Club in Washington, discussing the Navy's missions and policies. American officers abroad were not completely silent during this period. General John E. Hull, United States Commander in the Far East, made an important address to a luncheon meeting of the American-Japanese Society in Tokyo on October 23, in which he indicated that the United States had no desire to keep its forces in Japan indefinitely and that Japan must begin to provide for her own security as quickly as possible. On November 2, the Air Force Chief of Staff, General Nathan F. Twining, visiting Spain with Air Force Secretary Harold Talbott to discuss proposed United States air bases with Spanish officials, either said or was quoted as saying in the course of a press conference in Madrid that eventually all nations of the free world would be equipped with atomic weapons. Since this is not permitted by the terms of present atomic-energy legislation, the statement created a temporary stir in Washington and had to be appropriately "clarified."[49]

The pages of Congressional committee hearings and of the nation's newspapers in recent years have been filled with similar statements and accounts of similar activities. There is no doubt that one of the important indices of the emergence of American military officers as important leadership figures on the national scene is the greatly widening range and number of their public comments, statements, and testimony on important policy issues, presented to members of the Congress and to many public audiences.

Diplomatic Negotiations

Though not engaging in formal diplomatic negotiations, members of the Joint Chiefs of Staff and other high-ranking military officers have had increasing opportunities in recent years to talk to leading political as well as military figures in other countries in the course of their periodic inspection trips to various parts of the world. Visiting members of the Joint Chiefs seem to go through the same round of conferences and conversations in some countries as important Senators or Congressmen.

Mention has already been made of the diplomatic dimensions of the NATO Supreme Commander's role. To some extent he seems to be a sort of conscience as well as morale-builder for the NATO nations. Also previously noted was the substantial activity of civilian and military members of the Defense Establishment in the meetings of the NATO Council and its subordinate bodies, the Military Committee and the Standing Group.

As for direct diplomatic negotiations with other nations, the Korean truce negotiations provide one obvious example. The United Nations side was represented exclusively by military officers (all but one being American), but there was no rule which made this obligatory. Furthermore, as was pointed out earlier in this chapter, the negotiations leading to the grant of Spanish air and naval bases to the United States were carried on for the most part by missions of Air Force and Navy officers.

One of the most interesting examples in recent years of diplomatic activity by the military is provided by the complicated series of intra- and intergovernmental discussions and negotiations that led to the Treaty of Peace with Japan and the accompanying United States–Japan security treaty. From the time that a special State Department group headed by John Foster Dulles was established to take charge of the Japanese treaty problem, an Army colonel was attached to the Dulles group as a liaison officer between it and the Defense Department. This officer accompanied the Dulles group on all of its diplomatic trips—the negotiations at the United Nations in New York in the fall of 1950, trips to Japan and the Far East in January and April of 1951, and visits to London and Paris in June of that year. Dulles was also accompanied on his trip to Japan in January 1951 by Assistant Secretary of the Army E. D. Johnson and by the major general heading the Army's Civil Affairs Division. Johnson went along again when Dulles returned to Japan briefly in April 1951 as a result of the relief of MacArthur. There was one further diplomatic task to be accomplished after the signing of the peace treaty and the security treaty in September 1951, and that was the negotiation of the important Administrative Agreement that would provide the implementing details for the security treaty. This was put in charge of Special Ambassador Dean Rusk, who had just resigned as Assistant Secretary of State for Far Eastern Affairs, and he departed for Tokyo in January 1952. He was accompanied again by Assistant Secretary of the Army Johnson, and by a number of military officers and civilian experts from the Defense Establishment. When the agreement was satisfactorily worked out with the Japanese in late February 1952, both Johnson and Rusk signed it for the United States. This fact would seem to symbolize rather well the role played by Military Establishment members of this particular series of diplomatic missions, for all the available evidence indicates that they were full and active participants rather than mere window dressing.

Conclusion

The evidence presented in this chapter illustrates clearly the many and varied ways in which the American Military Establishment—its professional officer personnel as well as its civilian leaders—participates in the formulation and the carrying out of United States foreign policies and programs. The participation is widespread and substantial and to a considerable extent formalized and accepted as normal by the military officers and civilians involved, whether within or outside the Military Establishment. It has been one of the major characteristic features of the United States foreign-policy-making process since World War II and would seem to leave no doubt as to the substantial impact and "influence" of the military on the various phases and aspects of this process.

At the same time, such military activities raise some very important problems for the American nation. As already noted, there has been considerable discussion in the country about Military Establishment organization and about a "proper" role for the military in the making of national policy. Some of the factors that help to explain or justify military participation have been examined. In the next two chapters the expanded role of the military will be examined in terms of the American tradition of civil control and civilian supremacy, and its constitutional and institutional embodiments, in order to discover what particular problems and dangers emerge. It should then be possible to indicate some of the essential conditions under which necessary and effective but at the same time limited and circumscribed military participation and influence in national-policv-making can be maintained.

chapter four

The Problem of an Appropriate Role
for the Military

Civilian Supremacy: The Principle Examined

The principle of civilian supremacy, of military subordination to the civil power, is one of the more important underpinnings of the American democratic system. It is embedded in the Constitution, implemented in legislative statutes, and reflected in the administrative structure of the Federal Government. The relevant Constitutional provisions, some of the major legislation, and some of the essential administrative arrangements have been noted in earlier chapters. It remains then to examine more closely the meaning and implications of this traditional American principle.

Constitutional and Institutional Requirements

In brief, the principle would seem to mean that, both formally and *effectively*, the major policies and programs of government, whether in the foreign or domestic fields, whether of policy toward France, the development of atomic energy, or even the size of the armed forces, should be decided by the nation's politically responsible civilian leaders. The distinction between *formal* and *effective* is important and requires a word of explanation. *Formal* refers to the written rules—the Constitution, statutes, and administrative rulings as noted above—which are *designed* to establish conditions under which civilian supremacy is maintained. *Effective* refers to the application of the rules in such manner that the conditions of civilian supremacy are actually fulfilled. Formal rules usually provide only general guidance for policy-makers; hence the rules must be interpreted and supplemented. During the latter process, the formal rules may be obeyed technically, but the values intended to be protected by them may actually be undermined. It should also be noted that often a new set of rules may be established, through habit and requirements of particular situations, which are quite contrary to the formal rules. This is particularly true of the shift of the military role from expert adviser to representation referred to in the previous chapter.

In his *American Democracy and Military Power*, Louis Smith sets forth the formal requirements for democratic civil control in these terms:

1. The heads of the government are civilians and are the representatives of a majority of the citizens to whom they are accountable and by whom they may be removed by the normal functioning of existing legal and political processes;

52

2. The professional heads of the armed services are under the control of the civilian leadership of the government in a manner which is both constitutional and *effective*;

3. The departmental management of the military establishment is under the *authoritative* direction of civilians who co-ordinate all phases of the program, and are themselves responsible members of a responsible administration;

4. Elected representatives of the people make the general policies, including such things as the decision about war, the voting of money and men for military purposes, and the granting of whatever emergency powers are also required; also, they are able to exercise an ultimate and general control over those responsible for the execution of policy;

5. The courts are in a position to hold the military accountable for the protection of the basic democratic rights of the people of the nation.[50]

However, even in this essentially formal and legal formulation, Smith introduces the terms *effective* and *authoritative*.

A further and seemingly necessary concomitant of the principle of military subordination to the civil power is a nonpartisan, career-servant role for the professional officers of the Military Establishment. This means presumably that they will perform their assigned duties in the same way no matter what political group or party is in control of the government. In this sense, they are in the same category as so-called civil servants. They supposedly bear no political responsibility for the advice they give and the professional decisions they make. These are expected to be based solely on professional and technical considerations and thus can with reason reflect favorably or unfavorably on professional skills and qualifications. On the other hand, it is presumably out of bounds for them to dispute publicly the decisions of their politically responsible civilian superiors. On this basis there can of course be no questioning President Truman's right to relieve General MacArthur, whatever one's views on the substantive policy issues on which the two men differed. In fact, this "civil servant" role would seem to imply certain limits in general on what is desirable activity for the military officer. These and other questions of a similar kind will be discussed in Chapter Five.

The foregoing represent some of the essential Constitutional and institutional prescriptions and criteria for the maintenance of civilian control. The key question is whether these are in themselves sufficient to assure it. In order to answer this question, it would seem to be important to look more closely at the underlying rationale for civilian control and at the apparent nature of the contemporary military "threat" to American democracy.

The Rationale for Civil Control

To some extent, this principle is accepted without question as a part of the American ideological heritage. There are, however, a number of impressive practical arguments offered in support of its continuing importance. The essential rationale is rather obvious. A part of it was set forth in the discussion of the "military mind" in Chapter One. More broadly, what are thought of as "military" procedures, patterns of behavior and ways of thinking are regarded as definitely antithetical to or at least posing some threat to democratic values and institutions. One of the most important supporting arguments for this point of view is provided by the sharp contrast between the character and procedures of a military organization and what are thought of as democratic processes and procedures. Normally, decisions in a military organization are made without special attention to the preferences of the larger membership, or consultation with the members or their representatives. Orders proceed through a hierarchy consisting of sharply differentiated ranks. Unquestioning obedience to them is expected and is enforceable by appropriate disciplinary measures. The assumption is that men developed and promoted to high positions in such organizations will tend to stress the necessity of disciplined and orderly action, obedience, physical strength and courage, the welfare and security of the larger unit or group as against that of the individual member, and the ability and willingness to use violent means if necessary to obtain one's ends. The contrast with democratic procedures relying on individual initiative and consent, with the line of authority flowing in theory from the mass of the citizenry to the leaders at the top, and with the essential stress in the democratic value system on the voluntary, the individual, and the egalitarian is obvious.

It is these characteristics of military organization and their presumed consequences in the general orientation of the military officer that are disturbing. The fear is that expanding military influence in the making of major governmental decisions will result in policies and programs that tend increasingly to reflect the presumed military desire for obedience and discipline, a lack of attention to popular feelings and preferences, and a certain lack of respect for essential political and civil liberties. The placing of professional military men in positions of governmental power and influence outside the Defense Establishment is likely to have similar consequences, according to this view, because men who have been trained and have been successful in the armed services will presumably be characterized by these same "military" attitudes and patterns of behavior looked upon as threatening to democratic purposes and principles.

A second reason for suspicion and distrust of the military lies in the fact that they are the group in control of and most skilled in the use of the most effective weapons and techniques of violence possessed by the society. Clearly such a group, whether as an instrument of some clique, party, or demagogic leader or as the active leaders themselves, would have an excellent chance of imposing their will on the society, if perchance they could gain the support of their forces in such a venture. This is not suggested as an actual or impending threat to American democracy, but it is a possibility that the good democrat must occasionally ponder.

A further reason given for keeping the military "in their proper place"—and this relates primarily to foreign policy—is that they are more likely to recommend military tools and techniques as the instruments of policy, i.e., to suggest use of force or threat of force in American dealings with other states. As with some of the reasons already given, many observers would no doubt be inclined to register demurrers or at least qualifications. However, as Quincy Wright has suggested, military men would at least be inclined to have the same kind of biases and predispositions about the use of the skills and techniques of their own field as professionals and specialists in other fields.[51]

The fact that the military man is a professional, a specialist of sorts, provides a somewhat more general argument for keeping him under civilian control. Just as there is reluctance to let the economist, the psychologist, or the physicist have a controlling voice in the making of important policy decisions, so it is felt that the military man should be confined as far as possible to offering advice and suggesting and analyzing policy alternatives rather than being allowed to make the final policy decisions.

Furthermore, the military man is not *politically* responsible for the decisions he makes or strongly influences. He may have to answer to a Congressional committee, and he may be relieved of his command for a number of reasons, but he is not directly responsible to the citizenry for what he does. They cannot remove him from his post. Not being responsible in this sense, it is argued, he will tend not to be sensitive to the needs and feelings of the public. Some may suggest that this last characteristic is a source of strength, but with regard to important decisions, it is certainly not in accord with the principles and requisites of a democratic society.

The Nature of the Military "Threat"

Certainly not all students of the problem would accept the validity of these supporting arguments, or the preciseness of the brief characterizations of them presented here, but this discussion should suggest at least some of the practical considerations underlying the emphasis on civil control over the military as one of the fundamental principles of American democracy. It should also suggest that what is opposed or feared is not simply participation or influence of one degree or another by the military departments, or more particularly their professional military personnel, in the making of major governmental decisions.

No one will deny that military officers should give their advice and recommendations on certain policy problems facing the government. Neither will anyone object if such recommendations are accepted in some instances. It will also be conceded that it is difficult to draw the line between the giving of advice on the one hand and, on the other, insisting that it is absolutely necessary to pursue a certain course of action if disaster is to be avoided (assuming that the latter might be regarded as "inappropriate" behavior). In other words, under certain conditions, those who are giving expert advice may be in a position, as noted earlier, where it is almost impossible for their civilian superiors to reject it and thus may be providing in effect the essential shape of the decisions taken.

There is the additional fact that much, if not most, of the participation of military officers in the making of foreign policy is of the representational sort. If most of these activities are viewed as necessary or useful, few would suggest— or have suggested—that they be discontinued. Furthermore, while it is certainly possible to exclude the top-ranking professional officers of the Armed Services from the nation's high-level policy-making councils such as the National Security Council, it could hardly be seriously proposed that the high civilian officials of the Defense Establishment be excluded. It is not the civilian leaders of the Military Establishment who are usually viewed as a threat or a problem, but rather the professional officers of the Services. What then is to be done if, as has often been the case, the formal civilian superiors of these military officers are in effect little more than their "front men," acceptable spokesmen for presenting and supporting the views and preferences of the professional military?

The view being set forth here is that the participation per se of the professional military in high-level governmental policy-making is not, in essence, what is regarded as dangerous. It is rather those "military" attitudes, preferences, and patterns of thought and behavior which supposedly characterize the professional officer, and which, it is presumed, he brings with him into policy-making. In other words, it is essentially as the "carrier" of certain values and attitudes, as the possessor of a "military mind," that the military man becomes suspect. It is

perhaps a double threat that he seems to pose: first and probably most fundamental, to the democratic values and institutions of the society, and second, to
the achievement of reasonably well-balanced and not overaggressive or force-
oriented policy-making.

If this analysis makes sense, then it may be argued that insofar as such "military" qualities and characteristics are present or begin to develop among State
Department officials, Congressmen, and other civilian policy-makers (or among
the wider populace itself), this would represent as much of an extension of "military" influence, as much of a threat to civil supremacy, as the increasing admis-
sion of "military-minded" generals and admirals to the high councils of the
American government. In other words, it is possible to argue that the civil and
democratic character of American society might be subverted while the government was still legally and effectively controlled by politically responsible civilian
leaders. In short, civil supremacy may be undermined by civilian leaders. On the
other hand, from a more philosophic point of view civilian supremacy prevails
as long as the civilian leaders are formally and effectively making the major decisions. Thus it can be argued that a democratic society has the right to "doom
itself," to turn to a "garrison state," to authoritarianism and dictatorship, if it
voluntarily elects to do so. Whichever position one chooses, the preceding discussion would seem to make clear that meaningful civil control cannot be assured
solely by the existence of certain constitutional prescriptions and legislative
statutes.

It is interesting to note that Louis Smith, whose study of this problem is
set in a traditional constitutional framework, seems as much concerned with the
possible spread of military habits of thought and patterns of behavior through the
wider society as with the increasing powers and responsibilities given to the
American Military Establishment and its professional officers as a result of World
War II and the period of great international crisis and tension that has followed
it. Indeed, one of the possible dangers that he points to is the development of a
"garrison state" in this country, if the present international situation and the role
of the United States in it continue relatively unchanged for a considerable period
of time. What this concept (originally set forth by Harold Lasswell[52]) refers to,
in brief, is the society's arrival at a situation in which the "military" emphasis on
order, discipline, obedience, and the use of force and violence would tend to
take precedence over traditional liberties and democratic values. With regard to
Smith's point, it should be noted that he does not view the possible development of a garrison state as necessarily the product of malevolent design, whether
on the part of the military or of others who would use them as instruments. It is
viewed rather as something that might develop gradually, stemming from the
fears and anxieties produced by intense preoccupation with the security of the
nation over a considerable period of time.[53]

Smith's comments point to a number of important questions for which there
would seem to be no reasonably precise and satisfactory answers available at the
present time. For example, how far has the United States moved in the direction
of a "garrison state" in recent years? To what extent have these "military" patterns of thought and action just discussed been gaining ground within the American government, either through the increasing dominance of the career military
officers or through the spread of "military" attitudes to civilians both in and out
of government service? Another obvious and fundamental question is the extent
to which American professional military men, in their typical ways of acting and

thinking, actually do fit the stereotype of the military man that has been presented.

Meaningful Civil Control

It should be clear from this discussion that maintaining the primacy of the civilian point of view and of democratic values and procedures in the American government presents a much more difficult and complex problem than simply assuring that there are appropriate constitutional and institutional safeguards designed to control the nation's professional military officers. The notion of *control* itself may be misleading to the extent that it implies that what is needed to maintain civil supremacy is certain obvious and easily applied limits or restraints on the military. As has been suggested, it may not be only or largely the professional military officers who have to be "controlled." Also, the sort of controls that will be effective may be neither obvious nor easily applied. Even in Mr. Smith's list of five criteria for democratic civil control previously presented, which is essentially institutional and constitutional in its approach, the terms *effective* and *authoritative* are introduced. This would still seem to leave his set of criteria inadequate in terms of the analysis presented in this study, but it indicates his awareness that an appropriate governmental framework and administrative organization are not in themselves sufficient to ensure meaningful civil control.

Effective control and *authoritative* direction suggest, as should the whole of the preceding discussion, that civilian supremacy is going to depend essentially (trite as it may sound) on the quality of the Government's civilian leadership. Only to the extent that civilian leaders are committed to democratic values and procedures and the necessity for a civilian point of view can the requisite supremacy be maintained. Their intelligence and understanding, their clarity of purpose and direction, and their courage and confidence in the face of various anxieties and exigencies of a "cold war" and even of full-scale war itself seem to be crucial. Clearly, civilian leaders must look beyond the mere preservation of formalities to see whether their actual relationships with the military reflect the values symbolized by the formalities. In this sense, civilian apathy and ignorance may as effectively subvert civilian supremacy as a deliberate attempt by the military to augment their authority.

To repeat, there are no simple devices for gaining the kind of civil supremacy discussed here. Certainly there is much more involved than keeping the military departments, and more particularly their professional officer personnel, under certain constitutional restraints and a continuing civilian surveillance. This does not mean that the devices for control provided by the Constitution and legislative statute are unimportant and can be ignored, but rather that they can only be used effectively by civilian leaders who have the necessary will and understanding. What this involves in the area of foreign-policy-making will be pointed out in some detail in Chapter Five.

Other Relevant Factors and Criteria

In determining an appropriate role for the military in foreign-policy-making, there are other important factors to be considered besides the principle of civilian supremacy and its various implications. For one thing, as was demonstrated at some length in Chapter One, the need for the military's skills and services in the formulation and execution of United States foreign policies and programs seems to be undeniable. Few responsible observers would take exception to this view. In fact, the critical international position of the United States and the consequent need for military knowledge and expertness have led some people to say in effect: The paramount consideration is or should be the national security of the United States (usually not defined at all or not very clearly defined). Let's not worry about these subtleties and refinements of civilian supremacy; our system of government is sufficiently strong and stable. Let's concentrate on getting to work those people who can best do the job of defending American national security (and for many, this may mean the professional military). Those who argue this way are not usually antidemocratic or opposed to traditional American values and institutions. They are simply more concerned with national security under conditions where in their view survival in the military sense takes priority over all other values.

On the other hand, one of the assumptions of those concerned about the maintenance of civilian supremacy is that more desirable policies and programs will also be a consequence of vigorous civil control. In effect, they would argue that civil supremacy and increased national security will go hand in hand. But this would not necessarily seem to follow. No doubt if faced with the choice (presuming that it was a meaningful one) of greater risks to national security or to democratic civil control of the society, some of them might prefer to take their chances with the former.

Another relevant criterion is suggested by the terms *economy* and *effectiveness*. In his 1953 reorganization plan, President Eisenhower stressed the importance of making the most effective and economic use of American resources in providing for the national defense. This is, of course, an objective that no one will quarrel with in principle, but its implementation is often quite another story.

With regard to the problem at hand, the terms presumably mean, in general, making the most economical use of the Military Establishment's knowledge, skills, and resources in foreign-policy-making. It would also seem to imply reasonably clear and precise assignment of responsibilities (with the powers, resources, and coordination and communication devices appropriate thereto) in the foreign-policy field among the various agencies, civilian and military, involved.

With regard to these factors and criteria, the essential point to be made is that the problem of an appropriate role for the military in foreign-policy decision-making (and in other fields of national-policy-making as well) involves choices for the society—choices among competing preferences, or more likely, among various scales of priority with regard to such preferences. Some values may have to suffer at the expense of others. For example, the United States Government could decide to go along without any military skills or advice in foreign-policy-making, keep the military pretty tightly circumscribed and close to "strictly military" activities, preferring the possibly greater risk to national security that might thereby result in return for a lesser threat to democratic values and institutions. Or it could be argued that economy or efficiency are irrelevant or in any event far less important than guaranteeing adequate and more than adequate national security. Let's get the best possible national-security program with cost only a secondary concern. During 1953 and early 1954, some critics and observers were suggesting that the Eisenhower Administration had made something of an opposite choice and was prepared to take somewhat greater risks on national security for the sake of greater economy, or in any case, reduced governmental expenditures on national security. While, as suggested above, some people are so concerned with the phenomenon of "creeping militarism" that they are willing to take increased national-security risks in order to control it, there are others sufficiently worried about the inadequate state of national security to argue that there is too much civilian interference with the professional military in the latter's efforts on behalf of national defense, that this is hurting the American defense effort, and that therefore "creeping civilianism" is the threat to be guarded against!

However, as even this discussion of value conflicts and value priorities makes clear, there is a set of traditional American beliefs about the role of the military —beliefs about the importance of civil control and civilian supremacy to the maintenance of American democratic values and institutions—which still seems to be widely adhered to and accepted throughout the nation by both the civilians of the society and by the professional military officers themselves. The principle was strongly restated once again in the message to Congress that accompanied President Eisenhower's Military Establishment reorganization order. On the other hand, there is also widespread agreement on the need for substantial military participation in the making of both foreign and domestic policy, and of course, for the most economic and efficient possible national-security and foreign-policy program.

If one accepts, then, the notion that military participation in foreign-policy-making (1) *is necessary*, (2) *should be effective and economical*, and on the other hand (3) *should not threaten the values and institutions of American democracy represented by the principle of civilian supremacy*, then the essential question to be asked is What would seem to be the conditions conducive to achieving such military participation and activity? This is the subject of Chapter Five.

chapter five

Necessary, Effective, and Limited
Military Participation

This study has of course been primarily concerned with only one aspect of the problem of civil-military relations in a changing era. Although the present chapter will discuss the conditions prerequisite to a proper role of the military in foreign policy, it should be emphasized that the general analysis seems relevant to all areas of public policy in which civilians and military personnel participate jointly—notably civil defense, the atomic energy program, and mobilization of the economy for national defense.

Greater Civilian Clarity Concerning the Military Role

Military participation in foreign-policy-making places important burdens on civilian leaders and officials who need to be aware why, at any particular time or for any particular problem, the military are involved, whether they are acting as expert advisers or merely representing their department, and what it is that they are contributing or can contribute. Civilian leaders may sometimes even have to face up to the problem whether military participation is particularly necessary or desirable.

Vigorous Civilian Leadership

Doubtless an approach so authoritative must depend on vigorous and positive leadership by the top politically responsible civilian leaders—the President, the Secretary of State, the Secretary of Defense, and the major figures in the Senate and House of Representatives. Assignment of tasks in the foreign-policy field should be clear-cut and appropriate—appropriate to departmental skills, interests, and responsibilities. Important ambiguities, communications blocks, failures in coordination, and jurisdictional disputes must be recognized and corrected promptly.

Furthermore, if the State Department is accepted as the nation's and the President's department of foreign affairs,[54] as *primus inter pares* in the field of foreign policy, then its officials and policy-makers must presumably be ready to take the initiative in dealing with problems of foreign policy; they must be ready to lead, to coordinate, and to make sure that various economic, psychological, and military policies fit into the larger policy framework—the "grand strategy" or "master plan"—that is assumed to lie at the basis of United States foreign policies and programs.

In a recent book on American foreign policy, John J. McCloy, who as United States High Commissioner for Germany (a State Department position) from 1949 to 1952, and Assistant Secretary of War during World War II, has had considerable experience in dealing with practical problems of civilian-military relations, puts the matter this way:

Above all, we must have officials in the State Department who have political vision and the ability to foresee and act upon vital world problems. They must have the capacity to develop long-range programs for our security and that of the free world. Though they must have a full realization of the limitations which military and economic considerations impose, they must have courage, initiative and force in the political field. There must be a greater sense of the urgency of anticipating problems. They must be prepared to put forward creative proposals and they must not fold up at the first negative paper which emanates from the Pentagon, however formidably it is presented.[55]

An important illustration of how not to carry out this role of leadership in foreign policy is provided by the willingness, not to say eagerness, with which the State Department turned over the direct control of the defeated enemy countries to the Military Establishment. At least such is the way the actions of the Department looked to some critics. Others defend the Department as essentially a policy-formulating and -planning agency rather than one designed to carry out field programs itself, and thus wise to refuse this burden. That the Department tended to change its own mind on the matter is suggested by the fact that it did take over direct control from the Army in Germany in 1949. In any case it is difficult to see how the State Department can carry out its leadership role without taking the vigorous path prescribed by McCloy.

The foreign-policy activities with which this study is concerned take place within the complex organizational setting of the United States Government. Accordingly, the positive and vigorous civilian leadership called for must express itself in organizational and administrative decisions which pave the way for substantive decisions on foreign-policy programs.

Minimum Use of the Military to Legitimate Policy

The activities of the Military Establishment, and particularly its professional officers, in support of the broader foreign policies and programs of the Government were noted in some detail in Chapter Three. The pressures that have produced such practices are not difficult to understand. Some of these officers carry a weight of considerable prestige and respect in Congress and with the public. Their recommendations are likely to be heeded when those of some civilian official in the State Department or elsewhere are viewed critically and suspiciously. Given a situation in which an Administration regards the enactment of its policies and programs as a matter of considerable urgency, there is a strong temptation to make use of the high standing of these officers, a temptation felt even by those who understand what the disadvantages are. There is no tradition against the appearance of civil servants or military officers before Congressional committees; on the contrary such appearance is expected and demanded, and this fact provides still further justification for the practice.

Given traditional Congressional attitudes and procedures, it is obviously impossible to bar completely testimony before legislative committees by military officers. It is not even desirable. There are certainly aspects of many contemporary foreign-policy decisions that involve expert military knowledge—the military strength of this nation and of other nations, both friendly and hostile, the worthwhileness in military terms of helping to arm friendly nations, the desirability from a military viewpoint of having certain overseas bases, and in general the military gains, risks, and costs of any particular policy. In this realm perhaps General Omar Bradley is right in saying that the legislators are entitled to "as full and complete information" as the chief executive officers were given by the military before any decisions were made.[56] However, there comes a point where the military become advocates of some larger policy (which often has many implications and consequences going far beyond the military's special area of expertness or assigned responsibility) and where they are making supposedly expert judgments and evaluations in areas which would seem to lie outside their special competence. The consequences of widespread legitimating activities of this sort by the military, whether before Congress or in public addresses, seem or have seemed in the past sufficiently undesirable to argue for their definite minimization.

There are a number of these undesirable consequences, and some were alluded to briefly in Chapter One. For one thing, members of the Military Establishment have sometimes taken advantage of their policy-legitimating activities to argue a policy or a point of view different from that of the official position. What sometimes happens is that the military officer quite consciously uses the forum originally given to him to support the governmental policy in order to take issue with all or perhaps some aspect of it. Needless to say, legislators, particularly of the opposition party, are often not averse to encouraging the expression of such differences. Another form that such activity sometimes takes is a bit more subtle, but may be equally significant in its consequences. This is the more or less unconscious expression of disagreement with the official view which may stem from the enthusiasm or commitment of an officer to his assigned responsibility. For example, statements made by the NATO Supreme Commanders on occasion have seemed somewhat opposed to the official policy line taken by American leaders and those of the other NATO countries. The NATO Commander's commitment to his assigned task of assuring the best possible defense of Western Europe may lead him to make statements, propose courses of action, "lecture" the national political leaders who are presumably his superiors, and so on, in a manner which may be understandable but at the same time prove embarrassing or complicating for all concerned.

General Bradley's testimony on the Japanese Peace Treaty, discussed in Chapter Three,[57] suggests another undesirable consequence, namely, making the very difficult and complicated problems of foreign policy seem over simple and clear-cut by putting, in effect, a military or Joint Chiefs of Staff seal of approval on them. In the case of the Japanese Peace Treaty, for example, it may be asked whether the Joint Chiefs were the only or the most appropriate group capable of estimating the impact of the peace treaty and the three security treaties on peace and security in the Pacific. Were Special Ambassador Dulles and the State Department unaware of the relation of these treaties to United States security in the Pacific? This kind of situation emphasizes the need for greater clarity by all concerned with respect to the limited area of military expertise in these matters and the nature of the limits.

These are not unimportant factors. However, the basic difficulty posed by these legitimating activities of the professional military would seem to lie in the threat to the nonpartisan, career-servant character of their role, which still seems to be viewed generally as necessary and desirable. As noted among the "problems raised" in Chapter One, the essential question is whether the military can participate in a substantial way in foreign-policy-making without becoming so closely identified with policies or even political parties as to seriously threaten if not destroy their traditional role. If the nation's leading military experts and advisers become widely identified as political partisans, then what reliance is likely to be placed on the objectivity and expertness of their advice? All military advice may tend to become somewhat suspect in the eyes of one important political group or another. Military arguments and military issues may tend to be discussed in partisan political terms and emerge as political campaign issues, with military officers, military "experts," lined up on both sides of the argument. High-ranking officers of the Military Establishment whose plans and policies have not won favor within the Pentagon may seek outside political support for them.

That this is not just idle speculation is borne out by some recent events. For one thing, as noted in Chapter One, there were the severe, critical attacks on the judgment and objectivity of the Joint Chiefs of Staff by the late Senator Robert Taft in 1951 and 1952; also, the seemingly irresistible pressures on the Eisenhower Administration, from Taft and others, to appoint a completely new Joint Chiefs of Staff group, who would then take a "fresh look" at American military policy and strategy. Those civilian officials, military officers, and outside observers who have protested this politicizing of the Joint Chiefs would do well to face up to some of the recent developments that make the attitude of Taft and others at least understandable. Given the present situation of the American nation, there are a number of strong pressures working in the direction of the increasing political involvement of the country's top military officers, and not all of them are a result of the difficulties faced by the Administration in power at any particular moment. There are limits to what can be done. However, if there is general agreement on the desirability and worthwhileness of the nonpartisan, career-servant role of the professional military man, then it would seem to be incumbent on all of those concerned—Congressmen as well as executive leaders, Republicans as well as Democrats, the military officers as well as their civilian chiefs —to be more self-conscious about the role of the military, about what is to be expected from them, where they can make their most effective contributions, and what kinds of activities are most appropriate for them. An important contribution in this direction, it is suggested, would be minimizing their use in legitimating current major foreign policies and programs.

Greater Military Self-Awareness of Role Limitations

Again the comments that follow refer particularly to the professional officers of the Defense Establishment, since they are the career servants, the expert military advisers. The top civilian leaders in the Pentagon are, after all, political figures, politically appointed and politically responsible to the President and the Congress. They are going to be identified with the major foreign policies of the nation and share responsibility for them, and this is as it should be, given their particular roles.

The military officers as well as their civilian superiors and civilian colleagues should be self-conscious about the role assigned to them in governmental policy-making and the kind of limits it imposes on their public and official activities. It must be said that in general many if not most professional officers seem to accept and welcome the principle of civilian supremacy and the limited role prescribed for them in a democratic society. Generals Bradley and Eisenhower, among others, have on a number of occasions quite strongly stressed these principles and their acceptance of them.[58] While military officers are thus to some extent self-conscious about their role, this self-consciousness is not as widespread as it might be and is apparently not accompanied by very much clarity as to the precise nature and limits of the role.

Discretion in Public Utterances

This point would seem to be borne out by one noticeable behavior pattern of recent years. It is the tendency of certain high-ranking military officers to make public statements, remarks, or speeches on various foreign-policy issues with a seeming lack of discretion and sense of responsibility. In some cases, the issues commented on are still a matter of intragovernmental discussion and consideration. In others, the policies in question seem to be outside the range of authority and responsibility of the person making the statement. At times these remarks have actually seemed to contradict official government policy. It sometimes seems doubtful whether the statements have received appropriate clearance from the speaker's superiors.

There is no intention of implying that this lack of appropriate reticence and discretion in public is a characteristic only of certain military officers, although they have been among the outstanding offenders. On the contrary, this would seem to be a comment and a criticism applicable to many civilian officials both outside and within the military agencies.[59] Students of Congressional behavior might agree to the inclusion of a considerable number of Congressmen among the public officials referred to here.

The primary objection here raised is not to the making of foreign-policy statements by military or any other public officials per se, as long as the statements have been properly cleared or coordinated with superiors in the speaker's own organization and with such other agencies and officials as may be involved, and are agreed upon not only as accurate presentations of the official policy position but also as appropriate to be made at the particular time.

Why this restraint in public remarks is necessary should be quite clear. Conflicting statements on United States foreign policy, or statements that can be so interpreted, are likely to produce confusion, uncertainty, and even considerable anxiety and insecurity both in other countries and at home. It may imply or reveal conflicting views and purposes in what purports to be United States policy. The American governmental system imposes special difficulties in this regard; but at least within the executive branch it should be possible to achieve considerably more consistency and authority in the statements of public officials relating to the foreign policies of the United States Government.

A great many examples of public statements by military officers have already been provided, but most of these have been of the more responsible and restrained variety. In the less discrete category must be put many of the public remarks of General Douglas MacArthur and some recent speeches and statements by General James Van Fleet, made while both these officers were on active duty. Long before General MacArthur's publicly aired disagreement with the Truman Administration on United States policy in the Far East, he had revealed an inclination to set forth his views publicly on a wide range of subjects seemingly beyond his own area of responsibility as Supreme Commander for the Allied Powers in Japan (SCAP) and as United States Theater Commander in the Far

East. Through regular yearly pronouncements on such occasions as New Year's Day, the anniversary of the Japanese surrender, and the anniversary of the promulgation of the new Japanese constitution, and through other public statements, letters, and the like, the General presented his views on such questions as Japan's future role in the Far East, the readiness of Japan for a peace treaty, the nature of such a peace treaty, and still broader issues.[60] Even in terms of the wide discretionary powers granted to him, it would be fair to say that the General's public statements moved far beyond the bounds of what was necessary and appropriate in his role as SCAP and United States Theater Commander.

At the end of October 1952, General James A. Van Fleet, then commander of the Eighth Army in Korea, was quoted as saying:

> We need military victory. We must defeat the Chinese armies in the field. Korea is the key to Asia. Beating them is the only way to get back our prestige. We don't have to go all the way to the Yalu, but we must be prepared to hit the Manchurian air bases if we have to.[61]

Upon his return to the United States in early 1953, General Van Fleet reiterated before Congressional committees and in public speeches the same theme, that the only way to end the Korean War was by military victory. In addition, he charged that victory in Korea was almost in his grasp during the counteroffensive of June 1951, but that it was snatched away by the start of the truce talks at Panmunjom.[62]

These comments by General Van Fleet on the Korean War are interesting for a number of reasons. First, they point up again the close relation of military problems and decisions to larger foreign-policy issues. Second, they illustrate the seeming inability of some military commanders to see their military problems within such a framework of larger political and diplomatic problems. The theorem that "the only way to end a war is by military victory" is either true by definition, and therefore trivial, or of highly dubious validity if the key terms are carefully defined and appropriate attention is given to the larger political situation of which this war, or any war, must be a part. Finally, they provide another example of a military commander seeming to take public issue with the views and judgments of both his military and his civilian superiors.

It should be emphasized that neither the professional abilities nor the integrity of MacArthur, Van Fleet, and other officers who have a tendency to be less than reticent in public statements are being questioned—only their discretion and awareness of their responsibilities as participants in a complex governmental policy-making system. The military are not the sole or even the most important offenders. There seems good reason to argue generally for more discipline and restraint in public statements by American governmental officials, civilian as well as military, within the Defense Department and outside it, enforced if necessary by the top leaders of the government.

Refusal to Legitimate Policies

To return once again to the policy-legitimating activities of the military: if they were more aware of the limits imposed by their prescribed role, they would probably be more reluctant to become spokesmen for the larger policies of the Administration holding office, and thus there would be less of such activities. It may be objected that this awareness would have no effect at all, since the Secretary of Defense or the President can order military officers to testify if necessary. However, the political consequences of so ordering would probably be serious enough to make it quite unlikely to happen. Similarly, military self-consciousness of the sort suggested here should help professional officers to minimize in general, if they so desire, their involvement in partisan political issues and debates, ascription to them of political motives, their identification with particular parties and policies, and their being held in effect politically responsible for these policies.

Avoidance of Nonmilitary Problems

The military's lack of clarity about the nature of their role in foreign-policy-making also tends to lead them somewhat astray in another way. They have a tendency on occasion to get involved in questions and problems which do not concern them in any obvious or important way, and to which they can bring no special knowledge or competence. From the point of view of the most economic use of the limited human skills and resources available in the Government, such a tendency would seem to be undesirable.

While conceding the interrelatedness of many foreign policy problems (and many domestic problems as well!) it is clear that there are some problems of American foreign relations which are closely related to the use of military force or to questions of military strategy and military capabilities. Presumably these would be closest to the interests and skills of the professional military officer and the Military Establishment. Others have little or no direct relation to questions of military force or strategy, and thus presumably need not be a concern of the military. Examples of the latter might be the North Pacific fisheries problem and the agreement negotiated regarding it between the United States, Canada, and Japan; or more significant, the Point Four program of technical assistance to underdeveloped areas. Most problems of international trade and international economic stability would probably fall into this category, as would most of the technical and legal problems involved in the drafting of a peace treaty or other international agreements and conventions. Indeed, one of the criticisms that might be directed against the military in the case of the Japanese Peace Treaty is that they seemed to devote too much attention to and to be over concerned with matters of treaty wording that might safely have been left in the hands of State Department officers skilled in this kind of work.

Since there are limits to the organizational and intellectual resources of the military, it seems sensible for the latter to direct most of their attention to those foreign-policy problems in which the military dimension is of some significance. It would even seem appropriate for their civilian colleagues in the decision-making process to insist to the military that certain problems were rather far removed from their area of special knowledge and competence, that they were not inclined to pay too much attention to the views of the military on the quite obviously nonmilitary questions, and that the military might do well to devote their limited time and energy to the problems closest to the heart of their professional skills and concerns.

As has already been suggested, this general analysis would seem to apply with particular force to the activities of the Joint Chiefs. Since they are the body of military officers in the United States charged with strategic military planning at the highest level and with the broad strategic direction of the armed forces, it can be assumed that they are burdened with heavy and varied responsibilities, and inevitably have extremely limited time at their disposal. They should therefore not be spending time dealing with matters of small detail, with highly specific foreign policy and other problems and questions, as they have apparently done in the past. President Eisenhower's reorganization directive is in part an attempt to minimize the need for such activity, but perhaps the new Joint Chiefs of Staff group that took over in the summer of 1953 can take an important step toward their own more effective functioning (in their legislatively prescribed tasks) which does not involve organizational reform. This step is simply to gain a clearer notion of their role in the making of governmental decisions, and as one aspect of this, the kind of questions, problems, and matters of detail that are most economically and effectively dealt with at their level.

In sum, vigorous and imaginative civilian leadership, together with greater civilian and military self-consciousness about the nature and limits of the foreign-policy-making role of the Military Establishment and its professional officer personnel, should aid in the achievement of these fundamental goals: first, effective as well as formal civilian control of the major foreign policies and programs of the United States; second, more effective and economic use of the skills and resources of the Military Establishment in foreign-policy-making; and third, safeguarding the career-servant, nonpartisan role of the military officer in the American government.

Critical Scrutiny of the Military's Views

The comments that follow touch primarily upon the relationships and interactions in foreign-policy-making between military officers on the one hand and civilian officials representing civilian agencies on the other. There are at least two good reasons for this particular focus. First, the civilian official-military officer relationship is obviously a key one from the point of view of meaningful civil control. Second, it is probably the typical one in foreign-policy activities involving the Military Establishment and various civilian agencies. However, it should be clear that the general analysis is also applicable to civilian official–military officer relationships within the Pentagon, and in fact to the intellectual aspects of foreign-policy decision-making no matter who is involved.

Military Assumptions, Values, and Reasoning

Whatever the exact nature of the relationship between them, one of the most useful services that the civilian policy-maker can perform for his military colleagues is to make the latter more aware of the nature of their thought processes, of the preferences, assumptions, time perspectives, and lines of reasoning which presumably underlie their policy views and recommendations. Given the fact that many of the problems that the professional officers face at present in the foreign-policy field and many of the questions they are asked to deal with involve a wide range of factors lying outside the traditional areas of military knowledge and expertise, it is very important that the military be conscious of their professional and other biases in viewing various kinds of data and intelligence, and also of their basic assumptions and hypotheses about international politics. Equally important for military experts is awareness of the kinds of nonmilitary knowledge which they themselves must acquire or which must be obtained from civilian experts.

When the interdependence of military policy and foreign policy was discussed in Chapter One, it was indicated that the military could make meaningful recommendations on armament programs, overseas bases, and disposition of forces only within a framework provided by national objectives, policies, and resources, and also by assumptions and expectations about the capabilities and intentions of other nations. Once they move into this broader framework, however, they would seem to move outside the realm of their accepted and demonstrated skill and expertise. There would accordingly seem to be no reason to grant their views about these matters any special deference or consideration.

This does not mean that the military should arbitrarily be ruled out of the decision-making process at a certain point. Such would seem to be neither feasible nor sensible, given the nature and range of their responsibilities. Neither does it mean that particular views should be rejected out of hand because they are "military" views or advice, offered by military officers who are presumed to be illiterates in the political and economic realms. In fact, one of the developments that has to be faced up to by the civilian policy-maker is that there are some very skilled and sophisticated military statesmen within the armed services, whose insights and abilities in the politico-diplomatic field are probably equal to those of many capable civilian diplomats, administrators, and policy analysts. Nevertheless, once the military move beyond the ever-narrowing area in which they can claim exclusive skill and expertise to that much broader realm where political and military considerations are so closely related and intertwined that it is difficult to deal with them apart from each other, they should be on no more than an equal footing with civilian experts and policy-makers.

Some illustrations should help to clarify the point. The professional military staffs of the Armed Services may make certain policy recommendations relating to the scale of American rearmament, or to the desirability of obtaining certain military bases in Japan or Spain or French Morocco, or to the necessity for speedy German rearmament—recommendations which are based, or should be based, on estimates and assumptions about the capabilities and intentions of a number of other nations. What reason is there for assuming that such estimates and assumptions by the military will have any special validity or reliability as compared with those of skilled policy-makers and policy analysts in a number of civilian agencies? What justification would there be for accepting the military's analysis of the strengths and weaknesses in the social structure of the Soviet Union or of Soviet intentions and expectations in the foreign-policy field in preference to that of Russian experts both in and out of government service? The same question might be asked with regard to making any one year the "crisis year" in present cold-war tensions. There is certainly no basis on which predictions by the military as to the official and public reactions in various foreign countries to American policy decisions should be regarded as more trustworthy than those of civilian experts on such matters. Even more difficult and complex questions could be pointed to that must enter into the calculations of policy-makers, but these should suffice to make clear that foreign-policy decision-making involves many problems to whose solution the career military officer can bring no special claim of expertise.

It may be said that such questions are, admittedly, beyond the ken of the military, and that therefore what they are offering is "strictly military" judgments and estimates which do not attempt to deal with these "nonmilitary" factors and make no claim of doing so. This is quite clearly not the case. What does frequently happen is that the military will make certain policy recommendations or analyses which are labeled "military" or "strictly military," but actually rest on a series of unstated, inadequately stated, or perhaps not even clearly understood assumptions and hypotheses having little to do with purely military factors. These assumptions may range from notions about when and where a third world war is likely to start, or more generally, about the intentions of the Soviet leaders, to estimates about the viability of the Japanese economy, the durability of Communist rule in China, or the impact of German rearmament on opinion and stability in France. Clearly when General Omar Bradley talks about a full-scale war on the Asiatic mainland which might involve the United States as "the wrong war at the wrong place, at the wrong time, and with the wrong enemy," such an analysis is based, or should be based, on a clear and definite set of assumptions. If the set of assumptions and the line of reasoning that moves from the assumptions to recommendations of policy are made explicit, it should then be possible to find the specific bases for policy disagreements if there are such, to argue about the underlying assumptions or the time perspective in which the problem is being viewed, and perhaps to make some efforts to prove the validity of one set of assumptions as compared to another.

Military Time Perspectives

With regard to the question of time perspective, there is some evidence that the thinking of the professional military at least tends to equate a "military" or "strictly military" judgment or viewpoint with short-run maximization of the military security of the United States somewhat narrowly viewed. In the case of the peace treaty with Japan, for example, it is pretty clear that military preoccupation with safeguarding the operations in Korea tended to make the Pentagon somewhat reluctant about proceeding quickly with the peace treaty, even though it was regarded by civilian policy-makers as most important to the success of United States policy in Japan and the Far East.

If the military can be persuaded to make the time perspectives underlying their viewpoints explicit on all occasions, it would then be possible for the civilian policy-maker to question these, to disagree with the assumptions involved, to suggest that a policy decision which may tend to maximize the military security of the United States in one area for a relatively short period of time may, on the other hand, have some threatening implications for United States military security at some farther distant future date and over a wider geographic area. In other words, it might be emphasized that the long-run has its military, as well as its political and economic, costs and consequences. This is not to say that the short-run view, or the emphasis on military consequences, is always to be rejected out of hand, but simply that if the time perspective of a recommendation is made explicit, it should then be possible to attempt to strike a balance between short- and long-run consequences and implications.

Of course, it is possible that in some situations there is actually nothing that could pass for a more or less systematic and clearly thought out set of assumptions and analysis of alternatives underlying the recommendations made. One policy alternative is decided upon as desirable from the military viewpoint, for whatever reasons, and then so presented, either with no supporting arguments or rather unimpressive ones. This would seem to mean, in effect, that a situation was being viewed in something of a vacuum, with only certain factors of military strategy and tactics considered. In this case, it is difficult to see how such a recommendation can be regarded as anything more than the statement of a military textbook principle as to what such a situation calls for *in abstracto*. If a specific situation must be seen in terms of a broader context of events and purposes in order to be adequately understood and dealt with, it is difficult to see the usefulness of a recommendation that seems to ignore this context.

Louis Koenig suggests, in *The Sale of the Tankers* previously referred to, that one of the factors that may help to explain the slow progress made in arranging for the sale of the surplus United States tankers to foreign nations in that instance is that the governmental agencies dealing with the problem tended not to make their own underlying assumptions and reasoning processes clear or explicit nor to press other agencies for the ideas and information upon which they based their arguments.[63] The Joint Chiefs of Staff and the Navy Department were among the groups involved, and the Joint Chiefs' memoranda regarding the matter appeared to be dicta for which no supporting explanations and analyses were provided.

Legalism and Formalism in Military Thinking

As a further argument for critical scrutiny of the intellectual underpinnings of military views and recommendations, it should be kept in mind that the military have sometimes been accused of a rather legalistic and formalistic approach to international relations, not without a certain justification. There is a tendency in the thinking of some military officers to want always to be as legally safe as possible, to have the other party's commitments perfectly clear and precise, with no possible loopholes of wording or interpretation, while making as few such commitments oneself as possible. Another form in which this legalistic view of the world manifests itself sometimes is in the assumption that because another nation is in a position *in legal terms*—on the basis of some written agreement or the lack of one—to take actions that would be harmful or threatening to American interests, there is good reason to believe that these actions are more than likely to take place. Obviously, such an approach ignores the whole question of the particular nation's intentions and capabilities as well as the general nature of its relations with the United States. In addition, it also seems to ignore one of the more obvious lessons of recent history, namely, that when states are determined to take certain actions, they are able to provide themselves with appropriate legal pretexts or justifications, provided they are not inclined simply to bypass the whole question of legality. This preoccupation with being legally protected would seem to indicate either a lack of understanding of or a lack of confidence in the processes of diplomacy and negotiation between nations, particularly when their relations are more or less friendly. Certainly, to the extent that this legalistic-formalistic approach to foreign-policy problems is widespread among the professional military, the sort of critical approach to their views suggested here would seem to be even more appropriate and necessary.

It is important to note here that the tasks which are most generally assigned to the military—bases, occupations, training, weapon development, and so on—require concrete field operations. As implementers the military face innumerable everyday chores ranging from building of barracks to negotiating with foreign police officials. A continued experience of "getting things done" conditions thinking. The desire for directives, for precise rules, for clearly written understandings, is therefore not unnatural to the military man. He will tend to bring pressure to get matters settled, to arrive at explicit verbal formulations. All this may give the military the appearance of being practical men of action in contrast to the diplomat or policy analyst who deals with events in quite a different way and who must resist the temptation to reach rigid, inflexible solutions. Thus, the civilian and military perspectives are different because their tasks are different. The civilian policy-maker usually deals with situations and problems consisting primarily of social forces not easily evaluated or controlled. What may be regarded by the military as a hardheaded approach to such situations and problems may be, paradoxically, quite unrealistic.

The Military Mind Reconsidered

These comments are meant to be, and can only be, suggestive. As has already been emphasized, the question of the characteristics of military thinking at various levels in the organization of the armed services, with regard to foreign policy and other so-called civil problems, is a most important one in the field of civil-military relations and represents an area where considerable research is called for. Earlier in this study, an effort was made to suggest the reasons for the fear of military thinking. These were summed up in the notion of the "military mind." Here it must be emphasized that it is one thing to try to probe the qualities of military thinking which are relevant to the present problem, but it is quite another thing to lump these qualities uncritically under the impressionistic phrase "military mind." It would seem more fruitful instead to direct further inquiry about the characteristics of military thought to careful, systematic analysis of such factors as the motives, attitudes, perceptions, and intellectual skills of military personnel. In the light of information about these it may then be possible to determine whether there are qualities sufficiently common to most military officers to warrant speaking of a type distinguishable from the "business mind," the "bureaucratic mind," or the "American mind" (among others) and if so, whether any of these qualities seem particularly threatening or inappropriate in terms of the military's role in the making of national and of foreign policy.

There is an interesting and highly relevant British comment on the general problem that has been discussed in this section, a comment which seems worth quoting at length:

From Cardwell to Churchill, the British method of keeping the military under control has been to appoint experienced and energetic ministers who do not feel inhibited from imposing their veiws on the chiefs of staff on questions of military strategy as well as administration. Moreover, the hand of the minister is greatly strengthened by being a member of a Cabinet responsible to Parliament. But it has certainly not been lack of energy or experience which have prevented Mr. Forrestal and Mr. Lovett from being fully masters in their own house. The difference between London and Washington is not one of personalities, but of the attitude to military questions. The American services have successfully implanted the idea that there are such things as purely military factors and that questions which involve them cannot be adequately assessed by a civilian. British theory and experience denies both these propositions, and points triumphantly to the person of Mr. Churchill.

It is this difference in approach which accounts more than anything else for the current conflict of views between the British and American Chiefs of Staff over the size of the forces necessary to defend Western Europe. The British Government's paper suggesting that, with increased air power and atomic weapons, a considerably smaller number of ground troops than the 96 divisions originally envisaged would be sufficient to defend Western Europe from attack, fell with a dull thud in Washington some time ago. The Pentagon insists that the original figure was reached on sound military ground; there is a tendency to believe that the British Chiefs of Staff have allowed themselves to be influenced by economic and financial considerations which are irrelevant and that they are indulging in wishful thinking.

In part, of course, the argument is caused by different intelligence estimates of Russian strength, the British believing that the Americans have created an unreal monolith out of the Russian armies and are suffering from their habitual tendency to overinsure. But at bottom it stems from two different attitudes. The British staff officer who forms part of a closely knit team with civilian officials and politicians in Whitehall does not recognize the existence of a purely military argument. His American counterpart is prepared to take responsibility only for military factors and resents the intrusion of the civilian mind into any decision on their relative importance.

The incoming President has an opportunty to resolve not only this kind of problem, but also to adjust the whole relationship of military to economic and diplomatic strategy. President Truman, the man who grew out of a boy who wanted to go to West Point, has always been at a disadvantage in dealing with military men. Despite the bitterness of his political campaign against the General, he has always held them in awe.

President Eisenhower will come to office at a time when the conflicts between the Pentagon and the State Department may be very acute. The stalemate in Korea has created a recrudescence of the "give 'em hell" and "let's go it alone" philosophy among certain American commanders in the field. If France fails to ratify the European Defense Treaty the temptation to make a separate arrangement with the Germans will undoubtedly be strong both in the Pentagon and among its friends in Congress. If Mr. Eisenhower, newly turned civilian, can demonstate to his old colleagues in arms that he intends to refresh the principle of civilian supremacy, and also that military and diplomatic planning are only differing aspects of the same question, he will have done the western alliance a very good turn.[64]

This comment from *The Economist* reflects the general tone of the preceding analysis. There is no reason for civilian leaders and policy-makers to accept the policy recommendations of the military unhesitatingly and uncritically. At the risk of seeming to dilute the strength of this analysis, it must now be suggested that on the other hand there is similarly no reason for rejecting these recommendations. This is true even with regard to those military recommendations that might be termed "narrowly military"; that is, those which stress the factors closely related to military strength and military strategy at the expense of what might be called political, psychological, and economic factors.

The agreements for the establishment of United States air and naval bases in Spain provide a useful example. The obvious military advantages to be gained thereby in the form of additional secure bases in Western Europe and on the Mediterranean for the Navy and the Air Force presumably had to be weighed against the unfavorable effects on official and public opinion to be expected in various Western nations such as France and Great Britain, and the more general moral dilemma and burden of dealing with a Fascist dictatorship that had been in the enemy camp in World War II. All of this, of course, was in addition to the strong domestic political pressures on both sides of the issue. These are rather difficult matters to weigh and calculate, but it can at least be said that on close examination, the military desiderata are not so easily dismissed as those who think in stereotyped terms would lead us to believe.

This has been a much oversimplified discussion of this particular problem, but the general point would seem to be well taken—a "narrowly military" policy recommendation by the armed services should not be rejected out of hand. There may be foreign-policy situations where the elements of military force, military capabilities, or military strategy may be the most significant or the most useful. At the same time, it is clear that long-run advantages should not be sacrificed for short-run protection against rather unlikely military contingencies. As has been pointed out, the so-called economic and psychological factors may at some future time have very important implications for military strength and security.

It should further be noted that there is no suggestion in what has been said that the answers to many of these foreign-policy questions are simple, clear-cut, and obvious to the keen and dispassionate observer. All of these questions involve assumptions which are difficult to verify, situations which are changing quite rapidly, and complex combinations of factors and consequences which make it most difficult to take any path of policy action with full confidence and assurance. In rejecting one set of recommendations and choosing another there are, by definition, risks involved. But this is quite clearly a most risky world we live in. It is not possible to be free of risk, to be prepared to meet all possible contingencies successfully. The preceding discussion simply suggests that there is no reason for either accepting or rejecting on some a priori basis the military's ideas and advice on which risks or contingencies the country should prepare itself to meet.

Finally, it should be pointed out—and this is both obvious and fundamental—that the approach suggested in these pages would seem to call for and depend on a considerable amount of courage, self-confidence, and above all, intellectual skill, clarity, and imagination on the part of the civilian policy-makers and leaders. Admittedly, these are qualities not easily developed. Furthermore, civilian policy-makers do operate with important handicaps in certain areas. Earlier in this study it was suggested that one of the places at which civilian control may break down, even though explicit organizational checks supposedly operate, is where qualified civilian policy-makers feel under pressure to accept military information and interpretations—are in effect unable to reject them. What this suggests is that civilians should give some attention to improving their training in military lore, doctrine, and know-how. After all, the more recent military-training programs (as exemplified by the National War College) have apparently given military personnel some skills with which to scrutinize civilian thinking. Unless one is prepared to accept the notion that military organization and operations constitute an area of unique knowledge, perhaps the civilian official should be compelled to acquaint himself with military science. In this way, the courage, self-confidence, and intellectual abilities called for in dealing with the military might well be enhanced.

chapter six

Conclusions

The problem discussed in this study is not the only one in the realm of American foreign-policy-making. Its special importance arises from the uneasy condition of international politics and from the significance of new military techniques in contemporary statecraft. In a larger sense, the new role of the military and its consequences are symptomatic of the impact of revolutionary commitments and demands which now characterize American foreign relations. Since 1945 all kinds of stresses and strains have been imposed on the policy-making machinery. The various processes which generated foreign policies during the years when issues were relatively simple have undergone a painful, rapid, and far-reaching adaptation. During a short ten years the American people have experienced a reversal in the relative priority of foreign policy and domestic policy and have been confronted with the uncomfortable possibility that many of the virtues of their political system may have temporarily become troublesome, given the circumstances under which world leadership and responsibilities were thrust upon the United States.

Several of the major points which emerge from the preceding analysis apply—if they have been soundly argued—to the National Government in general, not just to foreign policy. Thus, the relationship between expert advisers and politically responsible officials is a significant one throughout the Federal structure. Likewise, the need for restraint and responsible behavior on the part of policy-makers is not localized in any one area of public policy, but is a requirement throughout all open, nontotalitarian political systems. Furthermore, politico-military decisions often require hard choices as to objectives and as to how scarce resources are to be used, choices which must ultimately be concurred in or supported by the American people as a whole. The same is true of any governmental decisions which involve truly national objectives and large expenditures of resources.

Emergence of military organizations and military leaders as key factors in political and social life is not confined to the United States, nor is it a novel phenomenon in the development of Western democratic societies. Therefore the present American problem is not unrelated to the past experience of nations whose cultural heritage is similar. For that matter, the role of the military in policy-making in nondemocratic regimes is relevant too. Recent shifts in the personnel and relationships of Soviet leadership do not appear to make much sense unless one takes into account the position of the Red Army. Scholars are now beginning to reconstruct the role of the military elite in the evolution and demise of German foreign policy from 1935 to 1945.

It is unfortunate that there is not available a systematic military history of Western civilization. Not very much is known even about the American experience since 1776. Such studies might be very helpful in assessing the conditions under which the military are invited to overstep, or overstep on their own initiative, the limits of their proper function, as well as the conditions under which their contribution to sound policies is either short-circuited or ignored. Perhaps historical studies would also help to put concrete meaning into the principle of civilian supremacy. The fact that extensive case reports on the contemporary role of the military in United States foreign policy are lacking means that it is difficult to avoid overemphasizing or underemphasizing the problems which have arisen. More accurate information would help the scholar, the citizen, and the policy-maker alike. Those farsighted military officers who have become increasingly aware of some of the difficulties of their position might, however, profit the most. Evidence from the recent German experience suggests that failure to structure the civil-military relationship properly, far from benefiting the career military officer, may have disastrous consequences for his professional position and prestige and also lead to national defeat.

Given the new international responsibilities of the United States and the probability of protracted world tensions, the governmental problem analyzed in this study will continue to require the serious attention of the American people for many years to come. Essentially, the problem which has arisen from the evolution of multiple forms of military participation in foreign-policy formation and execution is this: How can this participation be limited so that certain democratic values are preserved while at the same time the necessary military contributions to effective foreign policy are assured? From the standpoint of the substance of policy, the problem is: How can the armed strength of the nation be mobilized and used effectively as a servant of foreign policy over a long period of time without subversion of the structure of government, without threatening the economy, and without interfering with the realization of foreign-policy objectives?

This problem of policy process and policy substance is many-sided. It is, in short, a cluster of problems which are reflected in a number of situations and relationships—within the Military Establishment, between the Defense Department and the State Department (as well as other important civilian agencies), between the President and the Military Establishment, and between Congress and the Military Establishment. Perhaps the core problem is the maintenance of the Constitutional principle of civilian supremacy. In the last analysis, civilian supremacy must stand or fall not only in terms of the enforcement of formal rules and procedures, such as executive and legislative budget control, the executive appointment power, and allocation of responsibilities by law and so on, but in terms of the actual rules and procedures which govern civil-military relationships in numerous and diverse situations. To be meaningful, civilian supremacy must be precisely defined and defended, not as a formal principle, but in the actual conduct of civilian and military personnel as they jointly participate in policy formation.

So far as the content of foreign policy is concerned, the problem must be regarded as one of value conflict and priority. Military objectives may be incompatible with nonmilitary objectives, requiring an outright choice or assignment of priority. Selections must be made from competing techniques or strategies—

the use of military force versus diplomatic persuasion, or total military victory versus limited "police" action. Military techniques may affect nonmilitary objectives.

Another problem-within-a-problem, so to speak, is coordination. Military and civilian functions, information, and viewpoints—often very different in character —must be integrated in the course of policy formation and execution. The merging of the civilian and military elements in the policy-making process must be achieved under conditions which effectively preserve civilian supremacy. Difficulties of coordination such as communication failures, value conflicts, and jurisdictional rivalries will vary from relationship to relationship and will differ in part according to whether the military play an expert or representative role.

Basic to the question of an appropriate role for the military in foreign policy are the attitudes which civilian and military officials have toward each other and toward the two sets of roles involved. These attitudes will be a major determinant in the way civilian and military officials interpret the rules and procedures governing their relationships. Certain attitudes on the part of civilians can promote an extension of military influence which threatens civilian supremacy. Other civilian attitudes can render the necessary military contribution to foreign policy ineffective. Certain military and civilian attitudes may produce strong pressures toward the involvement of top military officers in party and factional strife, with the unfortunate consequence of politicizing career public servants.

A final perspective on the nature of the general problem under consideration is suggested by the fact that often civilian supremacy may be threatened or subverted without this being recognized by the participants in the joint relationship, and primarily as a result of unintended consequences of their actions.

An essential step in the solution of or adjustment to any social problem is an explicit common agreement as to its nature. One of the primary conclusions which emerge from this brief study is the necessity for careful and systematic analysis and for precise definitions of frequently used terms and concepts in dealing with the so-called "military problem." In one sense, the preceding pages have reflected an effort to explore the dimensions of a problem and to indicate the kind of knowledge required for understanding it and coping with it.

Just as the problem of a proper role for the military is really many-sided, so there is no one, neat formula for its solution. Formal rules and organizational reform per se are insufficient. Such checks must be reinforced by appropriate attitudes on the part of both civilian and military officials. In particular, both must achieve greater awareness of the nature of the problems which arise from their relationships, and greater clarity concerning the dimensions of their respective roles. The chief threat from the military is not the possibility of direct usurpation of power, but the inappropriate application of military values, information, and interpretations at key points in the decision-making process, and the phenomenon of "creeping militarism" among civilians. Indeed, the conclusion seems inescapable that civilian failures are the key to actual or potential military inroads on civilian supremacy. Ultimately, the major responsibility for establishing the conditions conducive to the necessary, effective, and limited participation of the military must rest on the top civilian leaders, including the President.

Thus civilians must insist upon role clarification, self-restraint, and nonmilitary education on the part of the military. Even more important, civilians must decide precisely what meaningful civilian supremacy is, in the various situations of joint military-civilian policy-making, and must be prepared to check the expansion of military functions beyond proper limits. If it is true that greater self-awareness and nonmilitary training are increasingly necessary for military leaders, it is equally true that civilians must be willing to exercise vigilance and to learn to evaluate military views.

In sum, adjustment to the problem of an expanded role of the military in American foreign policy requires new—and appropriate—attitudes and knowledge for military and civilian policy-makers alike.

Footnotes to the Study

1. See, for example, HANSON W. BALDWIN: "The Military Move In," Harper's Magazine, CXCV (December 1947), pp. 481–489.
2. A core list of the basic books and documents in this field is to be found in the Bibliographical Note. For a survey of current research, see WILLIAM T. R. FOX: "Civil-Military Relations Research: The SSRC Committee and Its Research Survey," World Politics, VI (January 1954), pp. 278–288.
3. For some interesting comments on traditional American attitudes toward the military and more recent developments in civil-military relationships, see HAROLD SPROUT: "Trends in the Traditional Relation between Military and Civilian," Proceedings of the American Philosophical Society, XCII, No. 4 (October 1948), pp. 264–270. A pioneer study in the field of civil-military relations is PENDLETON HERRING: The Impact of War (New York, Rinehart & Company, Inc., 1941).
4. Although this is a point of view that many Americans have only recently become aware of or adopted, it is really little more than a somewhat sophisticated and elaborated version of the oft-cited dictum about the close relation of war and politics, in Clausewitz's classic version, War is the continuation of political relations by other means. This is, of course, the Marxist-Leninist view, and its role in Soviet military thinking is discussed in Chapters 1 and 3 of RAYMOND L. GARTHOFF's recent book, Soviet Military Doctrine (Glencoe, Ill., The Free Press, 1953). It is interesting to note that according to Garthoff there is no study of the military doctrine (the "body of assumptions and beliefs about military science and art, strategy, and tactics which is accepted in any armed force as being the basic guide for its conduct of military affairs") of any other nations, similar to his work on the Soviet Union.
5. Section 101 (b), National Security Act of 1947 (Public Law 253, 80th Cong., 1st sess., July 26, 1947).
6. ARTHUR M. SCHLESINGER, JR.: "Military Force: How Much and Where?," The Reporter, IX (August 4, 1953), p. 13.
7. See The New York Times, April 9, 10, 16, and 21, and May 24, 1953.
8. ARTHUR W. MACMAHON: Administration in Foreign Affairs (University, Ala., University of Alabama Press, 1953), p. 27. Professor Macmahon has some excellent comments on the budgetary process as it relates to the national security program on pp. 26–33 of this volume.
9. SCHLESINGER: Op. cit., p. 15. For a good statement of the air-atomic approach to American national security see THOMAS K. FINLETTER: "A New Look at Air Policy," The Atlantic Monthly, CXCII (September 1953), pp. 25–30. Mr. Finletter was Secretary of the Air Force in the Truman administration.
10. See BERKNER's statements reported in The New York Times, May 2 and October 20, 1953. There is also an article by BERKNER on this subject (adapted from the speech reported in The New York Times on October 20), "Science and Military Power," Bulletin of the Atomic Scientists, IX (December 1953), pp. 359–365. For some more general comments on this and other problems of the age of atomic weapons, see J. ROBERT OPPENHEIMER: "Atomic Weapons and American Policy," Foreign Affairs, XXXI (July 1953), pp. 525–535.

11. The Brookings Institution: *The Administration of Foreign Affairs and Overseas Operations* (Washington, D.C., June 1951), p. 121.

12. These quotations appear in the following: BALDWIN: *Op. cit.*, p. 482; WILLIAM O. DOUGLAS: "Should We Fear the Military?" *Look*, XVI, No. 6 (March 11, 1952), p. 34; C. L. SULZBERGER: " 'Military Mind' Weighed as Political Question," *The New York Times News of the Week in Review*, June 1, 1952; ARTHUR M. SCHLESINGER, JR.: "Generals in Politics," *The Reporter*, VI, No. 7 (April 1, 1952), pp. 33–36; JOHN P. MARQUAND: "Inquiry Into the Military Mind," *The New York Times Magazine*, March 30, 1952, p. 53; and "The U. S. Military Mind," *Fortune*, XLV (February 1952), pp. 91 ff. Also worth looking at are JOHN J. McCLOY: "In Defense of the Army Mind," *Harper's Magazine* CXCIV (April 1947), pp. 341–344, and DREW MIDDLETON: "The Enigma Called 'The Military Mind,' " *The New York Times Magazine*, April 18, 1948, pp. 13 ff.

13. There is much useful information in Brookings Institution: *Op. cit.*, Chap. 5.

14. MACMAHON: *Op. cit.*, p. 21. This description covers the situation as of 1952.

15. See JOHN W. MASLAND: "The National War College and the Administration of Foreign Affairs," *Public Administration Review*, XII (Autumn 1952), pp. 267–275.

16. Section 211, National Security Act Amendments of 1949 (Public Law 216, 81st Cong., 1st sess., August 10, 1949).

17. The complete text of this speech is to be found in the *Department of State Bulletin*, March 16, 1953, pp. 412–416. The underscoring in the quotation is General Bradley's, not ours. This speech is interesting from several points of view. First there is the careful effort to explain the role of the Joint Chiefs of Staff in foreign-policy-making, which has been quoted. Second is the very fact of General Bradley's speaking on the question of war or peace in Korea (the subject of the address), which inevitably has implications and ramifications far beyond the realm of the military. Bradley shows rather impressive awareness of this fact and attempts to discuss the problem in the manner he himself recommends for the Joint Chiefs in the passage quoted. But the very fact that General Bradley made such a speech, and that it was then reprinted in full in the *Department of State Bulletin*, in itself points up some of the problems involved in the role of the Joint Chiefs in foreign-policy-making.

18. See the Report of the Task Force on the *National Security Organization* (Appendix G, prepared for the Commission on Organization of the Executive Branch of the Government, January 1949), pp. 66–70; also, Secretary Lovett's recommendations to President Truman for improvement and reorganization of the Military Establishment, as reported in *The New York Times*, January 9, 1953. Dr. Vannevar Bush has had some interesting comments to make on the Defense Establishment, and particularly the Joint Chiefs of Staff. See his article, "What's Wrong at the Pentagon," *Collier's*, December 27, 1952, pp. 31–35. Another article with some provocative comments on the Joint Chiefs of Staff, as well as on civilian control of the Military Establishment, the operation of the National Security Council, and the role of the State Department in national security planning, is JAMES A. PERKINS: "Administration of the National Security Program," *Public Administration Review*, XIII (Spring 1953), pp. 80–86.

19. MACMAHON: *Op. cit.*, pp. 13–15 and 17.

20. There is some extremely interesting analysis of the Joint Chiefs of Staff and their relations with the four civilian Secretaries in a recent article by Townsend Hoopes, a civilian official with wide government experience, particularly in the Pentagon. See T. HOOPES: "Civilian-Military Balance," *Yale Review*, XLIII (Winter 1954), pp. 218–234.

21. GORDON DEAN: *Report on the Atom* (New York, Alfred A. Knopf, Inc., 1953), pp. 139–140. In discussing continental air defense, BERKNER: *Op. cit.*, pp. 363–365, talks about "the complete failure in communication between the vigorous elements of the scientific community and our top military and political leaders," with major emphasis on the high-ranking military officers.

22. For the text of both these documents, see *The New York Times*, May 1, 1953.

23. Needless to say, this has not been the only goal of these reorganizations. Among the others have been increased standardization and improved joint activity in certain fields, such as research and procurement, more efficient utilization of manpower, and of course more tactically powerful forces in relation to the men and resources mobilized.

24. See the discussion in WALTER MILLIS (ed.): *The Forrestal Diaries* (New York, The Viking Press, Inc., 1951), pp. 36–38, 44–46, 130–132, and 213–216; and HENRY L. STIMSON and McGEORGE BUNDY: *On Active Service in Peace and War* (New York, Harper & Brothers, 1948), pp. 599–602.

25. See BURTON SAPIN: "The Role of the Military in Formulating the Japanese Peace Treaty," in GORDON B. TURNER (ed.): *A History of Military Affairs in Western Society Since the Eighteenth Century* (New York, Harcourt, Brace & Co., 1953), pp. 751–762. Unless otherwise documented, further references to the Japanese Peace Treaty in this study are based on this article.

26. *The Sale of the Tankers* by LOUIS W. KOENIG appears on pp. 445–532 of HAROLD STEIN (ed.): *Public Administration and Policy Development* (New York, Harcourt, Brace & Co., 1952). The case as a whole provides an interesting illustration of the complexity and interrelatedness of foreign-policy problems, even those that seem at first glance rather simple and clear-cut, and also the extent of interagency discussion and negotiation that is sometimes necessary to deal with them. In addition to the Navy Department and the Joint Chiefs of Staff, the State and Interior Departments, the Maritime Commission, the Executive Office of the President, and finally, Congressmen and Congressional committees were importantly involved.

27. The expert-representational distinction would seem to be a relevant and useful one for the whole area of civilian-military consultation and cooperation.

28. National Security Act of 1947, Sections 101 (a) and (b).

29. For further information on the National Security Council, see the relevant portions of the Brookings and Macmahon studies previously noted. There are some pertinent comments in PERKINS: *Op. cit.*, pp. 84–86. There is also a chapter on the National Security Council in JOHN FISCHER: *Master Plan U. S. A.* (New York, Harper & Brothers, 1951), Chap. 2, "Mr. Truman's Politburo." For an account of some of the more recent developments, see Anthony Leviero's dispatch to *The New York Times*, May 4, 1953.

30. MACMAHON: *Op. cit.*, p. 205. There is further interesting material in the whole chapter on "Interdepartmental Coordination" (pp. 164–211).

31. General Omar Bradley stated this as the opinion of the Joint Chiefs of Staff in the course of the Senate hearings called forth by MacArthur's relief (see U. S. Senate, Committees on Foreign Relations and Armed Services: *Hearings on Military Situation in the Far East*, 82nd Cong., 1st sess., 1951, Part 2, p. 732).

32. This is illustrated by the attention devoted to the occupied areas in the semiannual reports of the Secretary of the Army. See, for example, *Semiannual Report of the Secretary of the Army, July 1 to December 31, 1949* (U. S. Government Printing Office, Washington, D.C., 1950), pp. 156–161, and *Ibid.*, January 1 to June 30, 1950 (Washington, 1950), pp. 79–84, particularly the sections on Japan. These semiannual reports by the Army, Navy, and Air Force Secretaries were instituted in July 1949. They are submitted to the President by the Secretary of Defense along with his own report. These documents, particularly the major reports issued at midyear, provide further, useful illustration of the wide range of Military Establishment responsibilities and the importance of many of these in the foreign relations of the United States. They are well worth looking at for this reason.

33. For further discussion, see SAPIN: *Op. cit., passim.*

34. For some discussion of the question of whether the Military Establishment is best fitted to undertake such occupation duties, see JAMES L. McCAMY: *The Administration of Foreign Affairs* (New York, Alfred A. Knopf, Inc., 1950), Chap. 11; and the Brookings Institution: *Op. cit.*, pp. 146–150, 198–202, and 236–238. McCamy's comments are particularly interesting.

35. Quoted in MACMAHON: *Op. cit.*, pp. 132–133. Macmahon's comments on the military-assistance program in Europe, particularly its administrative aspects, are very useful. See pp. 122 and 132–137. For an excellent broad survey of United States military-assistance programs to foreign countries in the postwar period, see Part 5, "Military Assistance and Mutual Security," in WILLIAM A. BROWN, JR., and REDVERS OPIE: *American Foreign Assistance* (Washington, D.C., The Brookings Institution, 1953).

36. See the story in *The New York Times*, February 25, 1953.

37. For the text, see *Ibid.*, April 2, 1952.

38. *Ibid.*, September 3, 1952.

39. That this is not a hypothetical problem is borne out by the accounts of Clifton Daniel and Robert C. Doty (*The New York Times*, November 17, 1952) regarding the friction between American forces and their British and French "hosts."

40. The agreements establishing the conditions under which United States forces are to operate in foreign countries are worth looking at as an indication of the complexities faced by the Military Establishment in carrying out these responsibilities. See the following:
    (1) "An Agreement Regarding Status of Forces of Parties of the North Atlantic Treaty," U. S. Senate, 82nd Cong., 2nd sess., Executive T;
    (2) "Administrative Agreement" implementing the United States–Japan Security Treaty (reprinted in the *Department of State Bulletin*, March 10, 1952, pp. 382–390); and
    (3) "Convention on the Rights and Obligations of Foreign Forces and Their Members in the Federal Republic of Germany" and the related Finance Convention (see *Convention on Relations with the Federal Republic of Germany and a Protocol to the North Atlantic Treaty*, U. S. Senate, 82nd Cong., 2nd sess., Executives Q and R, pp. 89–150).

41. Reported in *The New York Times*, May 8, 1953.

42. See U. S. Senate, Committee on Foreign Relations: *Hearings on Japanese Peace Treaty and Other Treaties Relating to Security in the Pacific*, 82nd Cong., 2nd sess. (1952), pp. 17–18 and 21–25.

43. See U. S. Senate, Committee on Foreign Relations: *Hearings on the North Atlantic Treaty*, 81st Cong., 1st sess. (1949), pp. 285–288.

44. See the Senate hearings referred to in footnote 31. A useful reference on the relief of General MacArthur and relevant events that preceded and followed it is RICHARD ROVERE and ARTHUR M. SCHLESINGER, JR.: *The General and the President* (New York, Farrar, Straus & Young, Inc., 1951).

45. For the complete text, see *The New York Times*, May 23, 1952.

46. Reported in *Ibid.*, April 9, 1953.

47. See the stories in *Ibid.*, May 18 and 20, 1953.

48. For the text of this speech, see *Ibid.*, February 2, 1951.

49. These statements and speeches were all reported in *The New York Times*. See the issues of October 25, November 12, October 9, October 23, October 24, and November 3, 1953.

50. LOUIS SMITH: *American Democracy and Military Power* (Chicago, University of Chicago Press, 1951), p. 15. The underscoring is ours. Aside from the Smith book and the Kerwin volume cited below, there is very little contemporary literature on the civilian-supremacy principle. There are a few noteworthy comments in the following: WILLIAM R. TANSILL: *The Concept of Civil Supremacy Over the Military in the United States* (Public Affairs Bulletin No. 94, Legislative Reference Service, Library of Congress, Washington, D.C., February 1951) and LINDSAY ROGERS: "Civilian Control of Military Policy," *Foreign Affairs*, XVIII (January 1940), pp. 280–291. However, with the possible exception of Smith's study, there is no systematic analysis of the principle in any of these references.

51. QUINCY WRIGHT: "The Military and Foreign Policy," in JEROME G. KERWIN (ed.): *Civil-Military Relationships in American Life* (Chicago, University of Chicago Press, 1948), pp. 119–121.

52. For Professor Lasswell's elaboration of this concept, see his article, "The Garrison State and Specialists on Violence," reprinted in HAROLD D. LASSWELL: *The Analysis of Political Behavior* (London, Routledge & Kegan Paul, Ltd., 1948), pp. 146–157; and also Chap. 2 in Lasswell's *National Security and Individual Freedom* (New York, McGraw-Hill Book Co., 1950).

53. See the discussion in SMITH: *Op. cit.*, pp. 7–16.

54. See Arthur Macmahon's rather eloquent statement of this point of view in MACMAHON: *Op. cit.*, p. 56; and his further comments thereon on pp. 176–177.

55. JOHN J. McCLOY: *The Challenge to American Foreign Policy* (Cambridge, Harvard University Press, 1953), p. 51.

56. See his remarks quoted on p. 28, and cited above in footnote 17.

57. See above, p. 47.

58. See, for example, General Bradley's speech cited in footnote 17, and also General Eisenhower's famous letter announcing that he was not a candidate for the Presidency in 1948.

59. This is the point of view argued by WALTER LIPPMANN, who has given some attention to this question; see particularly his column of December 2, 1952, in the *Washington Post*. In this article, Lippmann comments: "Essentially the problem of discipline is to put an end to the practice by officials and by military men of talking out of turn." "Among the well-known and highly undesirable forms of talking out of turn there are the following: 1. Speeches and press interviews by unauthorized civilian officials and by military officers on the policies and the high strategy of U. S. foreign policy. In any other civilized government the practice, as we have had to endure it for the past few years, would be considered gross insubordination. . . ." Along the same line, see LINDSAY ROGERS: "Our Brass-Bound Foreign Policy," *The Reporter*, VII (October 28, 1952), pp. 14–16.

60. For a substantial sample of these statements, see Appendix F of Government Section, Supreme Commander for the Allied Powers, *Political Reorientation of Japan* (Washington, D.C., 1949), vol. 2, pp. 736–789. Many of these are well worth reading for their style, content, and their reflection of a man.

61. *The New York Times*, October 30, 1952.

62. See *Ibid.*, March 5, March 23, April 2, and April 11, 1953.

63. STEIN: Op. cit., pp. 472–473 and 494–495.

64. *The Economist*, November 22, 1952.

Bibliographical Note

This Note is meant to be suggestive and highly selective rather than comprehensive. The items referred to here are viewed as a "core" list, a useful introduction to some of the problems and questions treated in this study. It is supplemented to some extent by the books, articles, and documents mentioned in the footnotes.

Although it is set in a traditional constitutional and institutional framework and has a minimum of systematic analysis, LOUIS SMITH's *American Democracy and Military Power* (Chicago, University of Chicago Press, 1951) is still a useful introduction to the general problem of civil control over the military. Within its own frame of reference, it seems comprehensive and has a wealth of relevant historical illustration. The volume edited by JEROME G. KERWIN, *Civil-Military Relationships in American Life* (Chicago, University of Chicago Press, 1948) is less useful. *A History of Military Affairs in Western Society Since the Eighteenth Century* (New York, Harcourt, Brace & Co., 1953), edited by Professor GORDON B. TURNER of Princeton University and prepared for an ROTC military history course, has a great deal of interesting historical material on both American and European experiences in the area of civil-military relations, and the last three chapters have a number of interesting and not easily accessible selections dealing with some of the contemporary problems posed by the threat to American national security. HAROLD D. LASSWELL's *National Security and Individual Freedom* (New York, McGraw-Hill Book Co., 1950) is a stimulating assessment of the impact on major American social and political institutions of the present substantial military security program. The Committee on Civil-Military Relations Research of the Social Science Research Council has prepared *Civil-Military Relations: An Annotated Bibliography, 1940–1952* (New York, Columbia University Press, 1954). An interesting historical case study of civil-military relations in another democratic nation is provided by JERE C. KING's *Generals and Politicians* (Berkeley and Los Angeles, University of California Press, 1951), which deals with relations among the French Government, legislature, and military high command during World War I.

With regard to the organization of the Military Establishment, one essential item is the National Security Act of 1947 (*Public Law 253*, 80th Cong., 1st sess., July 26, 1947), as amended in 1949 (*Public Law 216*, 81st Cong., 1st sess., August 10, 1949). Another basic reference is the report of the Hoover Commission (Commission on Organization of the Executive Branch of the Government, *The National Security Organization, A Report to the Congress*, February 1949), and more particularly, its Task Force on the *National Security Organization* (Appendix G, prepared for the Commission on Organization of the Executive Branch of the Government, January 1949). The Task Force study is a very important and interesting document. So are the Eisenhower reorganization directive and the accompanying message to Congress referred to in the text. Of great interest with regard to the structure and functioning of the present-day Military Establishment and also the processes of contemporary governmental decision-making in general are the experiences of the first Secretary of Defense, James Forrestal, as recorded in *The Forrestal Diaries* (New York, The Viking Press, Inc., 1951), edited by WALTER MILLIS.

In the specific field of the military's role in foreign policy, there is a great deal of interesting description and suggestive analysis in ARTHUR W. MACMAHON'S *Administration in Foreign Affairs* (University, Ala., University of Alabama Press, 1953), perhaps the wisest of the recent books on the organizational aspects of United States foreign-policy-making. Chapter 2 in JOHN J. MCCLOY'S *The Challenge to American Foreign Policy* (Cambridge, Harvard University Press, 1953) is a very pertinent and interesting discussion of the role of the military by a public figure of wide experience. The Brookings Institution study, *The Administration of Foreign Affairs and Overseas Operations* (Washington, D.C., Government Printing Office, June 1951) contains a great deal of basic information about the administrative structure of American foreign-policy decision-making and analysis of some of the major problems regarding it. Chapter 5 deals with the Defense Department.

A useful general source of information about the attitudes, values, and thought processes of some of the military officers who have played important roles in wartime and postwar national-policy-making is provided by their memoirs. Among the outstanding ones are DWIGHT D. EISENHOWER'S *Crusade in Europe* (New York, Doubleday & Company, 1948), OMAR BRADLEY'S *A Soldier's Story* (New York, Henry Holt & Co., Inc., 1951), LUCIUS D. CLAY'S *Decision in Germany* (New York, Doubleday & Company, 1951), and ERNEST J. KING'S *Fleet Admiral King* (New York, W. W. Norton & Company, Inc., 1952).

The hearings of Congressional committees and subcommittees, both on substantive policy matters and on appropriations, are a most useful and important source of information on foreign policy and on military policy and organization (and indeed, on almost any problem relating to the American National Government). Some Senate hearings on substantive policy questions have been cited in the study. The hearings on the military situation in the Far East that developed from the relief of General MacArthur are particularly pertinent and interesting for the student of American foreign policy and the role of the Military Establishment therein (see footnote 31). Congressional control over the Military Establishment through the military budget and the appropriations process has been historically surveyed and analyzed in ELIAS HUZAR'S very useful volume, *The Purse and the Sword* (Ithaca, N.Y., Cornell University Press, 1950).

As a final note, the columns of HANSON W. BALDWIN, military editor of *The New York Times*, in that newspaper are often quite valuable in their analyses of the military aspects and implications of foreign-policy questions, the impact of new weapons on strategy and foreign policy, and developments within the Military Establishment itself. On occasion, the syndicated columns of WALTER LIPPMANN deal with some of these problems, as do the columns of JAMES RESTON of *The New York Times*.